Merry Christmas
Shayle,

Lots of Love
Brenda x

Dec '93.

Andrei Tarkovsky was born on 4 April 1932 in the Soviet Union and was the son of the celebrated poet and author Arseni Tarkovsky. In 1945 he joined a school in Moscow which specialized in art (where one of his contemporaries was the poet Andrei Voznesensky). He enrolled at the Oriental Institute in 1951 but left two years later to join an expedition. He successfully applied to enter the Institute of Cinematography, VGIK, in 1954 and joined the directors' course supervised by Mikhail Romm, graduating in 1960. Later he taught at the Higher Courses in Film Direction in Moscow.

Tarkovsky visited Italy in 1980 to prepare a project which eventually became *Nostalgia*. On 10 July 1984, he announced in Milan that he would not return to the USSR since he had received inadequate assurances about his professional and personal future. Thereafter, he lived in Italy, Germany and Paris. He died in Paris on 29 December 1986, leaving a son and his widow, Larissa, who had worked with him on all his films since *Mirror*. His films include *Ivan's Childhood*, *Solaris*, *Stalker*, and *The Sacrifice*, which was released in the year of his death.

Kitty Hunter Blair translated Andrei Tarkovsky's book on the cinema, *Sculpting in Time* (1985), and his diaries for the years 1970–86, entitled *Time within Time* (1991). In collaboration with Jeremy Brooks she has translated plays by Ostrovsky, Chekhov, Gorky and Solzhenitsyn for the Royal Shakespeare Company, and works by Tolstoy, Dostoevsky and Chekhov for the BBC. She teaches Russian at Cambridge.

Philip Strick, MA, critic and film historian, secured the first London opening and British release of Tarkovsky's *Solaris* in May 1973. Former head of Film Distribution at the British Film Institute and deputy chairman of the BFI Production Board, he was managing director of the 16mm film library Harris Films for a number of years, and an extra-mural lecturer for London University. He is an overseas speaker on film topics for the British Council.

by the same author

SCULPTING IN TIME
Translated by Kitty Hunter Blair

also published by Faber

TARKOVSKY: CINEMA AS POETRY
by Maya Turovskaya
Translated by Natasha Ward
Edited and with an Introduction by Ian Christie

Andrei Rublëv
ANDREI TARKOVSKY

Translated by
Kitty Hunter Blair
with an Introduction by
Philip Strick

faber and faber
LONDON · BOSTON

First published in 1991 by
Faber and Faber Limited
3 Queen Square London WC1N 3AU

Photoset by Parker Typesetting Service, Leicester
Printed in Great Britain by Clays Ltd, St Ives plc

Photographic stills reproduced by kind permission of Artificial Eye Films

A CIP record for this book
is available from the British Library

ISBN 0-571-16376-9

Contents

The Re-shaping of Rublëv

Tarkovsky's *Andrei Rublëv* is a film that has changed its shape over the years. First unveiled in Moscow in 1966 as *The Passion of Andrei*, at 200 minutes it was almost an hour longer than the version which appeared seven years later at the Academy Cinema in London. What was missing, and why, became a matter for guesswork and rumour, fuelled by reports from Moscow and recollections of a showing at the 1969 Cannes Film Festival – presented out of competition, *Andrei Rublëv* was awarded a FIPRESCI prize by the international critics for whatever its screenplay consisted of at the time.

London audiences, faced with a historical pageant that stuttered fitfully through the first quarter of Russia's fifteenth century in a series of disconnected incidents of violence, rhetoric and unsignalled fantasy, could only assume that what had been cut was, in all probability, most of the story, as well as unimaginable quantities of material that might be interpreted as anti-Soviet in nature. Respectful recognition granted that what was left of *Rublëv*, although obscured and fragmented like the painter's icons themselves, still had an extraordinary potency.

Since then, Tarkovsky has become resoundingly better known, and the shape of *Andrei Rublëv* has been changed simply by the way we look at it – the film's anguished protagonist and the pauses and evasions of its structure now anticipate the familiar tones of the director's later work. At the same time, the re-release of *Rublëv* in versions closer to the original length (Tarkovsky's own preference, it is claimed, was for a 183-minute version which trimmed the opening and closing of several scenes and abbreviated the more violent episodes) has revealed that many of the gulfs in the narrative are deliberate, that the unheralded lapses into recollection or reverie are part of Tarkovsky's usual uninhibitedly associative style, and that what has been left mysterious and unexplored is so because it is either irrelevant or unknowable.

Never one to encourage interpretation, and impatient with

criticism at any level (although even he was to admit, in his book *Sculpting in Time*, that *Rublëv* 'strikes me today as disjointed and incoherent'), Tarkovsky asserted many times that his films should be accepted at face value, not dissected for their supposed meanings. With its dream-like dislocations, *Rublëv* both substantiates and contradicts this contention, in that its self-justifying impressionism contains a wealth of rational information: the more the film is examined the more its intricate meanings make sense – and the clearer Tarkovsky's achievement becomes.

With the publication of the film's original screenplay, here available in English for the first time, *Andrei Rublëv* changes shape again. This is not, like most screenplays, a dialogue list sprinkled with hints of background, nor, more elaborately, a shot-by-shot description of everything that happens in the film plus a few afterthoughts. Beyond expectation, this is an alternative *Rublëv*, the story freshly told by the same story-teller, its main events extended and rearranged, its detail altered in nearly every particular, its characters fleshed out with a richness and clarity the more remarkable for being almost entirely consistent with how they eventually appeared on screen.

It is a welcome bonus to find not only that Tarkovsky wrote in images with the same precision as when he filmed them but also that he wrote with such subtlety and balance. His story unfolds vividly through film-like descriptions on which the faces and places of the completed *Andrei Rublëv* unavoidably impose themselves, but like any novel of worth – even one which clamours, as this does, for translation into film – it has its own pattern, its own integrity, its own 'look'. As might be hoped, the text fills in a number of the gaps that Tarkovsky, as film-maker, prefers to leave open. But the main light that it throws is on what Tarkovsky was prepared to jettison from this (or any) script in order to reach the special qualities of 'pure' cinema. 'If a scene has been devised intellectually, following the tenets of literature,' he said in *Sculpting in Time*, 'then no matter how conscientiously and convincingly it is done it will still leave the audience cold.' The literary form of *Andrei Rublëv* illustrates a warmth, however, for which Tarkovsky repeatedly found a powerful filmic paraphrase of equivalent, or higher, temperature.

Tarkovsky's first draft for *Rublëv* was written after a decade of unsettled wandering and research. He had entered the Institute of

Oriental Studies in Moscow in 1951 at the age of nineteen, only to abandon the course in favour of an eighteen-month geological expedition to Russia's far north. When he returned to Moscow in 1954 it was in order to find ways of reacting to his experiences; film studies at the State Institute of Cinematography (VGIK) provided an acceptable route. Under the guidance of Mikhail Romm, who had worked with Eisenstein, Tarkovsky absorbed a solid diet of film classics, learned the declamatory visual language of the contemporary Russian 'masters' (a formidable roster including Bondarchuk, Kozintsev, Chukhrai and Kalatozov) and recycled them into his first feature film, *Ivan's Childhood*, which won the Golden Lion – the first Russian film ever to do so – at the Venice Film Festival in 1962.

The success of *Ivan's Childhood*, which was received as an elegiac war film in the tradition of *Ballad of a Soldier* and *The Cranes are Flying*, left Tarkovsky dissatisfied. He felt he had produced little more than a copy of conventional Russian cinema, an anthology of influences in which his own contribution had become stifled and insignificant. For a time he considered giving up film-making altogether, and it was in this state of uncertainty that he shaped the *Rublëv* project, a vastly ambitious epic that only the current hero of the Russian film industry, the Venice prizewinner, could have had a hope of securing the resources for, should he decide to go ahead. For him, it had the attraction of being entirely fresh while dealing with an unassailably Russian theme: it was not a matter of looking for something popular, respectable, or officially approved – Tarkovsky was simply not interested in non-Russian subjects. Emerging from the question of what kind of man would have produced the icons later recognized (by Church Council decree in 1551) as the peak to which all art should aspire, the *Rublëv* story had several attractions. One was that its setting would be the homelands to which Tarkovsky was profoundly devoted. More acutely, it offered the prospect of examining the causes and consequences of his own artistic dilemma.

Although describing Rublëv as 'a complete mystery', and having 'no intention of unravelling the riddle of his life', Tarkovsky provides a scrupulous historical context to the screenplay. He opens with the Kulikovo battleground where the Prince of Moscow, Dimitrii Donskoi, defeated the Tartar Khan Mamai in 1380; Kulikovo was a turning-point in the struggle to extract Russia from the control of the so-called Golden Horde, the western part of the Mongol Empire, but another century would pass before the final Tartar invasion was routed by Ivan III in 1481. Rublëv's lifetime, from c.1370 to c.1430, was a period of protracted chaos in which the Tartars attacked repeatedly (Moscow, then an outpost against them, was itself plundered twice), often encouraged by Russian factions ruthlessly fighting each other. Against this background of unrelieved brutality and hopelessness, succinctly expressed in Tarkovsky's proposed introductory images, the only comfort was religious faith. Churches were obsessively built and decorated, inspiring an upsurge of iconic artistry that was encouraged not only by the Russian nobility (as much for prestige as from piety) but also, oddly, by the Tartars themselves.

In the 1390s, Rublëv appears to have been associated with the Holy Trinity Monastery at Zagorsk, some fifty miles north-east of Moscow. The monastery's patron was Sergius of Radonezh, who was the spiritual adviser to Dimitri Donskoi in his stand against the Tartars and was later proclaimed a saint; the most famous of Rublëv's works, the *Old Testament Trinity* (now preserved at the Tretiakov Gallery in Moscow) was dedicated to the memory of St Sergius. After helping to decorate the Cathedral of the Dormition in Zvenigorod (a few miles to the west of Moscow), by 1400 Rublëv was a member of the Andronnikov Monastery in Moscow itself, and in 1405 he was summoned to help Theophanes the Greek decorate the Cathedral of the Annunciation there. Three years later he was in Vladimir, over a hundred miles to the east, working on the Cathedral of the Dormition. His later years were spent at Andronnikov, a teaching base from which he emerged for various assignments. His influence was such that icons surviving from the period reflect his style whether he had a hand in them or not, making the full extent of his activities the more difficult to measure.

When Dimitri Donskoi died in 1389, having claimed the title of Grand Prince of Russia, his elder son Vassily inherited the leadership, jealously opposed by another son, Yuri, based at Zvenigorod. The rivalry between the two princes provides the Rublëv story with a complex background to which Tarkovsky responds with relish and a profusion of factual detail. There is a limit to the amount of explanatory conversation that can realistically take place between the characters, but in both script and film

Tarkovsky – despite later doubts – has been intricately consistent except, perhaps, in the elision of chapters 6 and 8 of his screenplay to form the 'Last Judgement' chapter of the film in which the Grand Prince's mansion and the cathedral at Vladimir become strangely fused into one thanks to a well-concealed flashback.

Within this same chapter Tarkovsky includes a further complication: Rublëv's anguished debate as to whether to break with tradition in his designs for the cathedral. It is the aspect of the painter's life that had particular parallels with the film-maker's own predicament, and again it is based firmly on the evidence of the period. Byzantine art, brought to fourteenth-century Russia by the icons of Theophanes the Greek, demanded an inflexibly formal system of religious representation, with each saintly image accorded its specific location on the walls of every church. Rublëv's icons, while clearly derived from Theophanes' stern precepts, improvised a use of line and colour that eased the formalism into a gentler and more graceful mood, with details which (as Tarkovsky suggests in his final chapter) were probably inspired by the artist's personal environment.

Although a further identifiable stage of iconic development was to follow Rublëv's innovations, his work was the pivot on which Byzantine art turned into Russian, providing a model which, by Church decree, was faithfully copied from then on. The 'riddle' of Rublëv's personality lies in his originality of vision and his firmness of faith in a period when both were fiercely challenged; that Tarkovsky accurately perceived these as appropriate contemporary issues was ironically confirmed by the Soviet newspaper campaign which, in 1967, condemned both him and his film for an odd assortment of crimes including cruelty, naturalism, anti-patriotism, and 'religiosity'. Tarkovsky found such charges inexplicable and protested vigorously for the rest of his life that he had been wilfully misunderstood, and his films suppressed, by Goskino, the Soviet cinema organization. After *Rublëv* he made, with increasing difficulty, three further films in Russia before moving to the West in a form of self-exile; three years after his death in Paris in December 1986, *The Passion of Andrei* was showing again in Moscow, now hailed as his finest film and courageously autobiographical in spirit.

Tarkovsky in fact preferred to avoid being too closely identified with Rublëv, admitting only to the artist's 'dependence on nature' as a direct link. He saw himself, he said, as more like the bell-maker, Boriska, who bluffs and bullies a large team of assistants through innumerable hardships and great effort to help him create something of which only he pretends to know the secret, and which could easily prove a disaster. 'To count in advance on success,' said the film-maker, very reasonably, 'to calculate or foresee communication with the spectator, seems to me infinitely more risky than fidelity to oneself.' Nevertheless, it is Boriska's gamble (an elaborate enough enterprise as described in the screenplay but transcended by its staging for the screen where the giant bell makes a dominating presence) that rekindles Rublёv's urge towards creativity, subtly anticipated in the preceding scenes in which he fumbles with the same elemental materials that Boriska will use – charcoal and clay, fire and water. One suspects that Boriska's appeal, for Tarkovsky, is that he is an artist by accident and instinct, while Rublёv, more arduously but also more like all the central characters of Tarkovsky's work, questions, quantifies, and deeply distrusts each of his own decisions.

There are interesting comparisons to be drawn between the Rublёv of the text and the Rublёv of the screen after Tarkovsky's original chapters (and double preface) had been reduced to eight (plus prologue and epilogue). The script confirms, for example, that whether or not the monk was physically seduced by a 'witch' during the pagan festival, it is his mental sin that requires atonement. His adoption of the simple-minded peasant girl, who reminds him of the 'witch' (on screen the two actresses closely resemble each other), is part of a long struggle against worldliness that he can never quite win, and perhaps never should. But the script makes no mention of Rublёv's major crime on screen (or, to be accurate, just off-screen, since Tarkovsky is puzzlingly coy about staging it): his killing of a Tartar who attacks the girl during the assault on the cathedral. It is this action of complicity, even more than his horror at the general depravity of human nature, that prompts Rublёv's vow of silence – with the result that the film, much assisted by the actor Solonitsyn's eloquent discomfiture, shows the monk as more passionate and fallible, more self-regarding than at first conceived. More, too, is made on screen of Rublёv's relationship with his fellow monks; his reconciliation with his former teacher, Daniil, which contributes to the film's implicit sub-text of compulsive paternalism, was evidently a later addition.

In the script of *Rublëv* so much takes place that some other version of the film, twice the length, might fascinatingly have shown us – the comical peasants struggling with paint-boards in the streets of Moscow, Rublëv's first reaction to Theophanes' icons, the Grand Prince's secret tunnel, the dreams of flying, the memories of swimming, the squabbling column of blinded men, the miraculous scene in which the girl gives birth and recovers her sanity. There is an extraordinary moment when snow drops from a frame of scaffolding, another when ice-floes sweep past on the river, one bearing a jubilant drunk – moments that went unfilmed but remain powerfully framed in the mind's eye. Woven through the story is the account of a siege of Moscow when the Tartars demanded two cartloads of hair from the Russian women as the price for sparing the town. An incident barely mentioned in the film, it haunts the screenplay – and Rublëv's imagination – until, with a grand inevitability, it materializes at last in the climactic celebration of his paintings.

The horses, Tarkovsky's own icons, unite every chapter from Kulikovo to the final river bank; the film includes them with less vehemence, probably wisely, but the obsessive, unused image of the raven-black mare flashing across the years remains an indelible punctuation. Written with a grandeur that defies filming, the sequence of the swan-hunt illustrates the period in a manner Tarkovsky made no attempt to match with the camera. Instead, the completed film discloses a single bird-corpse and, in the scene of the Grand Prince's visit of inspection, a gentle blizzard of swan's feathers, drifting like snow or thistledown – which at times they seem to become – across scorched timbers like emblems of a forgotten past. Such images echo the text in a wonderfully improbable evocation, as if the book, once written, had been set aside and begun afresh, prompted simply by memory.

When it *was* re-written and pared down to a shooting-script, Tarkovsky shared the task with Andrei Mikhalkov-Konchalovsky, a fellow VGIK graduate who collaborated on Tarkovsky's two short diploma films (as did the cameraman for *Rublëv*, Vadim Yusov) and had a bit-part in *Ivan's Childhood*. Konchalovsky's career was to take him to Hollywood and an increasingly anonymous output of efficient action thrillers like *Runaway Train* and *Tango & Cash*, but his film *The First Teacher*, made in 1965 while Tarkovsky was in the midst of the three-year production schedule for *Rublëv*, certainly showed traces of Tarkovsky's influence. Both *Rublëv* and *The First Teacher* centre on an idealist whose tenacity wins out over brutal opposition, and there are superficial resemblances in the use of primitive communities, horsemen and landscapes. 'One of the things we were aiming for in our work', Tarkovsky and Konchalovsky said of their joint *Rublëv* script, 'was to recreate the real world of the fifteenth century for the audiences of today . . . to show, through the eyes of a poet, that wonderful and terrible age when the great Russian nation was taking form and shape.' It was indeed to be through the eyes of a poet, finally, that Tarkovsky made the Rublëv story unarguably his own on screen. In the following pages, we are privileged to have access to the poetic inner version that inspired it.

Philip Strick
May 1991

ANDREI RUBLËV

Andrei Rublëv was released in the USSR by Mosfilm in 1966. The film was awarded the International Critics Award at Cannes in 1969.

The cast and crew were as follows:

ANDREI RUBLËV	Anatoli Solonitsyn
KIRILL	Ivan Lapikov
DANIIL THE BLACK	Nikolai Grinko
THEOPHANES THE GREEK	Nikolai Sergeyev
DEAF AND DUMB GIRL	Irma Raush Tarkovskaya
BORISKA	Nikolai Burlyaev
BUFFOON	Rolan Bykov
PATRIKEI	Yuri Nikulin
FOMA	Mikhail Kononov
GRAND PRINCE	Yuri Nazarov
Sound	E. Zelentsova
Music	Vyacheslav Ovchinnikov
Art Direction	Evgeni Cherniaev
Editor	Ludmila Feganova
Photography	Vadim Yusov
Screenplay	Andrei Tarkovsky
	Andrei Mikhalkov-Konchalovsky*
Director	Andrei Tarkovsky

*Mikhalkov-Konchalovsky collaborated on the screenplay of *Andrei Rublëv* at the dialogue stage. The version published here is Tarkovsky's original *kino-roman* – see Translator's Note.

Andrei Rublëv is distributed in the UK by the Artificial Eye Film Company.

Translator's Note

Note on Transliteration
Proper names have been transliterated according to the Library of Congress system, since that can now be considered standard in this country. The only inconsistency is the British Library practice of retaining the final -sky for surnames already well-established in English with that spelling (rather than the awkward -skii which the Library of Congress system requires).

There are a few letters which require clarification for the reader unfamiliar with the Russian alphabet, since their pronunciation is not immediately obvious. The following list gives approximate equivalents of the sounds in question:

ë = yo in yonder
i = ee in meet; after a vowel i is comparable to English post-vocalic y
   as in boy, say
u = oo in hoot
y = i in hit

The Kino-Roman
The *kino-roman*, or screen novel, a well-established convention in Soviet and Polish cinema, is in effect a present-tense novel written as a first, prose version of the film. It is the basis for the screenplay or shooting-script which will be used by the director during filming.

Kitty Hunter Blair

Foreword

Age-old hatred swirls up into the torrid sky – clangour of steel, neighing, moans of the dying – and falls lifeless into the dust, beneath horses' hooves, a warrior, his face covered in blood.

Riders are unseated, curved swords gleam in the suffocating crush of battle, princely standards bend over, weighed down by Tartar arrows. Shouts, horror, death. Canvas shirts black with blood, shaved heads pierced with arrows, red shields split by axes, a horse thrashing about on its back, its belly slit open; dust, cries, death.

And just as the Russians are on the point of yielding to the weight of Tartar cavalry, Bobrok's mounted division comes flying out of the forest, speeds over the field, hooves barely touching the ground, falls upon the Tartar, crushes him, and pursues him over the field; red standards flutter over the white horsemen, and the Tartar, crazed with fear, falls with his horse in a cloud of dust . . .

The Field of Kulikovo, covered in corpses, fades into the gloom of night as if losing consciousness.

Dawn. Mist stretches out along the banks.

In the silence of the steppe, strewn with dead, the clip-clop of hooves rings out. A Russian soldier struggles to open his eyes. He is gravely wounded. A Tartar comes riding slowly over the field, through the mist, on a raven-black mare. The Russian raises himself, groping with the last of his strength in a pool of cold, slithery blood, till his hand comes upon his fallen sword; but his eyes grow dark, and he falls, unconscious, face down.

The Tartar's horse shudders, shies, and gallops away across the steppe, the frantic sound of its hooves echoing over the still waters of the Don. An arrow protrudes from the Tartar's chest. It is many hours since he was killed. The horse carried his corpse out of yesterday's battle, but only now does he fall to the ground, and his raven mare gallops on at full tilt towards the sun.

Prologue

The monk, Andrei Rublëv, sits in silence, leaning against a wall.

He hears snatches of conversation; the wind singing under the thatched eaves; the rustle of twigs; the drumming of hooves on the wooden floor of the stable; the full-throated, happy cry of swallows in the evening air.

His eyes are filled with helpless anguish, like someone who has suddenly lost the power of speech at the very moment when he is about to say something terribly important, something crucial to everyone who might hear it.

Deep in thought, Andrei listens with melancholy curiosity to the many voices of the world around him . . .

Along one side of the monastery courtyard, close to the endless stone wall, runs a sweating, dishevelled peasant. He is carrying a pair of wooden wings, and is pursued by an enraged, motley crowd of peasants, children, women and monks. They are shouting and throwing stones at him. One skinny monk, as pale as paper and breathless with the exertion of running, utters curses.

The peasant, not looking behind him, runs on towards the cathedral that stands at the far end of the flagged courtyard.

The crowd have all but caught him, but he throws himself into the open doorway of the church, leaping over the steps, and dashes off under the echoing arches, lost in cold and darkness, and then, darting on to the spiral staircase, goes twisting and turning up the steep, worn steps.

Down below, the voices of his pursuers thunder and boom. Pushing, jostling, swearing, they come pounding after him.

The peasant is already at the very top of the belfry. With frenzied haste he puts on the wings, fixing them to his back with specially made straps, and crawls out along the shaky railings.

The hostile crowd rage below him. Hundreds of people, hundreds of yelling throats, cries and curses.

The peasant spreads his wings, and, thrusting himself off, leaps from the bell-tower.

The crowd gasp, fall silent, and split into two parts, making a passage for the man to fly over.

He is flying over the earth, like an angel.

He sees rivers and fields, a small white church on a hilltop, surrounded by shiny-leaved birches, the graveyard with its leaning crosses, a burst of ripples on sunlit water, peasants haymaking, moving waist-deep in bright grasses, women gathering corn. They look tiny from up here, from this unapproachable, miraculous height.

He sees blue and dove-grey waves rolling smoothly away from one another, further and further into the distance, till they reach the line between sky and earth; huts, clinging to sloping hillsides; flocks on damp meadows plunged in shadow; yellow cornfields faded in the sun, falling and rising in the wind like waves; soft, dusty roads with little islands of untrampled grass, winding over fields and alongside rivers, meandering through bristly, curly-topped woods, among russet, red or yellow fields, and turquoise meadows.

He sees his own earth, where he was born and where he will die, and he sees it as no one has ever seen it before, and is unlikely to see it again.

The winged peasant disappears behind the forest.

People sink to their knees, dumbfounded by the manifest, priceless sanctity of this man who has flown away into the sky.

Crashing wings and limbs and branches, the peasant falls through a radiant white birch grove and dies as he hits the ground, his bloody, smiling face thrown back, so that the evening sun is turned to glass in his mischievous eyes.

Deep in the birch grove appears a black horse. Its nostrils quiver, it rolls its eyes and whinnies softly, frightened by the sight of the dead man.

1 The Buffoon: Summer 1400

A brilliant morning. Mist rises from the woods, and birds' wings, transparent in the sunlight, flash among the branches.

The gates in the wooden palisade around the Monastery of the Trinity are open, and two waggons loaded with huge barrels slowly make their way in. The small, shaggy horses are in a lather, for it is hard work; they keep going down on their hind legs and twisting the weight of the front axles and wheels now to the right, now to the left, to ease the load.

Three figures are walking down the road from the monastery towards the meadows: Kirill, aged thirty, Black Daniil, aged forty, and twenty-three-year-old Andrei. All three wear black workaday cassocks, faded by the sun and worn.

In the gateway appears a novice whose hair has not yet had time to grow long. His small, frightened eyes dart about, and as he sees the monks going off into the distance he shouts after them, purple-faced, in a piercing treble: 'Father Superior says you're to come back! He's asking you! He says there's no one can paint ikons in the Trinity! For God's sake, he says!'

The three stop.

'All right, now!' answers Kirill. 'On you go! It's none of your business!'

'You'll be sorry!' shouts the zealous brother, with unexpected venom, 'and when you come throwing yourself at his feet, he won't forgive you, the Abbot won't.'

'All right, all right, that's as may be . . .' Kirill answers, vaguely but with a note of anger.

'Stop it, Kirill, let's go,' Daniil interrupts him.

The monks walk slowly down the road.

The wooden palisade and the bell-tower of the Trinity grow smaller and smaller, and the hill on which the monastery stands seems to grow higher and higher.

*

It is hot and sultry. Andrei, Kirill and Daniil walk through water meadows, still unmown and thick with fibrous sorrel, clumps of camomile, and clover. They are following a well-trodden path, white in the sunlight, that runs along above the river.

Far away on the horizon the sky is no longer transparent, it touches the earth in a washy, dove-coloured mist thickening into cloud.

A thunder storm is gathering. For a while the sun still shines through a hot, stifling, milky veil, then it vanishes behind a cloud, heavy and dark as graphite, which is creeping stealthily across the dull sky. The monks walk in silence, oppressed by the heavy air and the coming storm.

'Where are we going to spend the night?' asks Kirill lazily.

'Don't know,' Daniil barely manages to reply. 'We'll see.'

'It's about to rain,' murmurs Andrei, with an enquiring glance at his companions.

'Andrei, you didn't come across a squirrel tail, did you?' asks Daniil. 'A little one, quite old?'

'No . . .'

'I've got it,' says Kirill. 'It was lying around on the window-sill behind a ladle.'

'Have you? I was worried. I'm used to it, it's good for trying out colours.'

'It's not good,' says Andrei with a sigh.

'What?' asks Daniil.

'Our leaving the Trinity . . .'

'Well, would it be better if we were buying and selling like our Abbott?' remarks Kirill. 'Go in for dealing in honey and bread? Eh? They're going to be trading in the church soon . . . Shopkeepers.'

'It'll be better in Moscow,' says Daniil.

'You always do that,' Kirill goes on, 'first one thing, then another, then a third. Seven Fridays in the week.'

For a while no one says anything.

'We did all decide together.' Daniil brings the conversation abruptly to an end, glancing sharply at Kirill.

They walk on in the thundery half-light that presages the storm, past haystacks, full of flowers, scattered along the edge of the wood. Suddenly Andrei smiles, but crossly.

'It just seems a pity.' He glances at the sky, shifts his pack to the

10

other shoulder, and, suddenly delighted, goes on: 'There, it's started spitting! I somehow don't think I shall ever come back here again.'

Smiling, Andrei walks on through the haystacks, gazing up and stretching out his hand to the long-awaited rain that is starting to fall in tiny, half-hearted drops.

'Yes . . .' Daniil concurs, 'look at this birch tree, for instance. You can walk past it practically every day without noticing it, then you realize you're not going to see it again, and look at it standing there . . . the beauty.'

'Indeed,' says Andrei. 'Ten years.'

'Nine.' Kirill corrects him.

'Nine in your case, ten in mine.'

'Not at all. I've been here seven years, you've been nine.'

Andrei's lips move; he is thinking about the years spent at the Trinity.

'There'll be plenty of painters in Moscow without us; won't there, Daniil?' Kirill turns to the older man.

'All the same, we'll find some sort of work. And even if we are of no use to them, they will be of use to us. I tell you, you only have to see Theophanes the Greek to have something to think about for the rest of your life.'

'Yes, of course,' says Andrei with a smile, 'but all the same, it's sad somehow, you feel some regret, don't you?'

It is starting to rain harder, and the monks quicken their step.

They pass a tree from which is dangling a hanged man. The corpse swings in the wind, its canvas shirt, wet with rain, flapping about its knees.

All three cross themselves.

'Andrei.' Kirill laughs suddenly. 'Could you kill a man for two roubles?'

Andrei does not answer, but keeps turning as he walks, glancing at the terrible tree.

'Do not trouble the heart of one who is already grieving,' says Daniil with a smile.

'That was never the result of a good life,' says Andrei.

Emerging from the wood they walk on in the rain, through the fields, further and further, along the wet path.

There is a roll of thunder, the sky grows as dark as at nightfall, and the rain drums down on the travellers' backs; they run along the slithery road, holding up the hems of their soaked cassocks, clumsily jumping over puddles, in the direction of a village that can just be glimpsed through the dense veil of rain.

And here is the village; the very first hut has a structure built on that is part shed and part parlour; the floor is of tightly packed clay, and one wall, hung with harnesses, scythes, and pitchforks, is also of clay, and whitewashed.

In the centre of the shed a puny little man with a disproportionately large head is standing on his hands, twitching his legs and squealing like a piglet. His shirt has slipped down, covering his face and revealing a dirty, sunken belly.

By the wall, on hay and on a dung-strewn bench, several peasants are sitting. Next to the bench stands a bucket of beer with a ladle. The peasants are laughing loudly, clapping their hands and shouting.

At the sight of the monks they all fall silent, the buffoon drops to his feet and jumps up, hurriedly straightening his shirt and looking anxiously at the newcomers.

One of the peasants, evidently the man of the house, stands up.

After a pause he asks quietly, 'What do you want?'

'It's raining . . . we just want to wait here for a bit,' says Daniil.

Without a word the host picks some crumbs from his beard, looks gloomily across from the buffoon, seated cross-legged on the hay, to the silent peasants, and then at the monks who are standing in the doorway against a luxuriant mass of raindrops.

'We shan't be in your way, we'll just wait for it to ease up. You go on . . .'

The man of the house smiles cautiously, and then boldly asks: 'Maybe you'll take some beer? Look at you, you're soaked.'

'We don't drink,' answers Kirill, politely. 'Thank you.'

The monks sit down in a corner.

Outside the door the rain beats down relentlessly, whipping up bubbles which sail slowly in the wind on the muddy puddles.

The buffoon takes his bag from the bench and begins to make ready to leave – he packs his tambourine and the other simple tools of his trade. He seems embarrassed, avoids looking at anyone, and is breathing heavily, thick drops of sweat hanging from his long, hooked nose.

'Where are you off to?' asks someone in surprise.

'Have to be on my way,' answers the buffoon, clearing his throat, with a sidelong glance at the monks. 'Thank you for your courtesy, I'll be off.'

The brothers in their wet cassocks are sitting under the window, helping themselves to the food they have laid out on the table, and seem to be taking no notice of anyone else.

'What do you mean? Wait a bit,' says a cheerful red-haired peasant, quickly walking over to the anxious buffoon and trying to dispel the atmosphere of suspicion and mistrust. 'Here, have another drink!' And he offers him a ladle full of beer.

The buffoon looks questioningly at their host, who, overcoming his own uncertainty, nods with affected indifference: 'Go on, go on, drink up!' – and he sits down on the bench with the others.

The buffoon takes the ladle and drinks, obediently and cheerfully.

'And now let's have it all over again from the beginning!' shouts the convivial redhead, heartily, and the others visibly cheer up, all ready to start watching and listening once more.

The buffoon wipes his mouth, smiles like a child, takes his tambourine from his bag, and walks out to the middle of the room.

He waits for them to be silent, strikes a sharp blow on the tambourine, and starts to sing in a high, piercing voice about a goat whose beard was shaved off, and of how sorry he feels for the unfortunate beast who was so ashamed that he had to hide himself in back gardens.

The song speeds up, the words turn into a tongue-twister and then, when they have virtually lost all meaning, sound like an incantation.

It is so compelling that the peasants begin to beat time, and even when the words are completely unintelligible the men go on laughing because the buffoon pulls such extraordinary faces, and is so comic as he limps and jumps, imitating the goat, that the meaning is clear without words.

The dance grows faster, the buffoon keeps banging the tambourine, striking it on his knees or on his forehead, or making it produce a steady sound that grows louder and louder.

He goes capering around the barn like a goat. And the men, clapping their hands, helpless with laughter; the walls hung with collars, bridles and sickles; the small window, open on to torrents of rain; the three monks in the corner; the buffoon himself in his flapping linen shirt with his ceaseless flow of sounds and high jinks – all merge into a wild, frenzied giddy-go-round.

The buffoon jumps on to a peasant's lap, from there on to the bench, from the bench through a mid-air somersault down on to the floor, grabbing a wisp of hay and twisting it around his head, creeping like a wolf while they all roar with laughter; suddenly he switches from a growl to a gripping, hysterical whisper accompanied by tense jingling on the tambourine, fraught and mysterious; and then, with a yell, he leaps up, pulls down his trousers, and, to the uncontrollable laughter of his helpless audience, he shows them all his scraggy, white behind.

That is the climax.

Last of all, the buffoon jumps on to his hands, and, flailing his legs, utters a shrill, piglet squeal.

Tired and drenched, he rises slowly from the floor, goes over to the door, kicks it open, and walks down the porch steps; pulling his shirt off over his head he exposes his bony back to the rain, and stands motionless for a while, gazing into the grey, rainy sky.

Highly satisfied, the peasants wipe their flushed hot faces with their sleeves, wag their heads and chat together, recovering their equilibrium after that stunning spectacle.

'What a player! A master, a real master!'

'How did it end then? Eh? Did I miss something? Eh?'

'What were you bellowing about then?'

'It was funny.'

'Well then, that was it. What d'you mean – did you miss something? You Smolensk bumpkin, you!' a small thickset peasant says in superior tones to his puzzled neighbour, and goes out into the yard.

The man from Smolensk gets up and follows him in silence.

'What's brought him here from Smolensk?' the red-haired peasant asks the host.

'Things are hard there, he says. You work away, ploughing, sowing, and that, and suddenly – back come the Tartars and there's nothing to eat.'

'Well, and what about here? They come here often enough, don't they?'

14

'He says they get them three times a year over there.'

'Go on!'

'Go on yourself. You ask him then, if you don't believe me.'

Andrei looks at the buffoon's pale back, the shoulder-blades protruding under the lashing rain like a pair of axes, the thin, boyish neck, the back of his head; and he waits impatiently for him to turn round.

At last the buffoon puts on his shirt and comes back indoors. It is hard to recognize him as he walks into the barn: he seems to have aged by ten years, he stoops like an old man, and his expression, as he glances around, is weary and sad.

Andrei's eyes meet his, and he realizes that the buffoon's thoughts are somewhere very far away, and that he is terribly alone in the wide world.

'Yes . . . God gave the priest, and the devil gave the buffoon,' mutters Kirill.

No longer wanted, the buffoon sits down in the hay beside his bag. For a time he is silent, staring down at the earth, then he takes his psaltery out of the bag, settles himself more comfortably on the floor, and begins to sing, barely touching the mournful, humming strings.

The peasants have already forgotten about him; but now they stop talking, and listen.

The buffoon is staring at Andrei without seeing him, and singing a beautiful, ancient song. The simple, naïve words make it sound extraordinarily mournful and pure. The buffoon is singing the song for himself, and perhaps also for others whose souls are no less burdened with sorrow than his own. His gaze is steady and expectant, as if he can see into another's thoughts, and Andrei lowers his eyes.

The peasants listen, enchanted, to the wonderful song.

Kirill scrutinizes the buffoon with distaste; the peasants are carried away by the song; Daniil and Andrei are entranced and full of excitement. And Kirill quietly gets up and slips out of the barn into the rain.

The buffoon's voice is soft and slightly hoarse. The song, merging with the sound of the rain, becomes utterly desolate.

Suddenly there is a dull thud against the wall and a desperate cry. The song breaks off.

Andrei dashes to the door and flings it open, and they all see two

15

peasants fighting together, in the pouring rain, in the thick soft mud of the yard. One of them staggers to his feet, having clearly been felled by a blow, and the other, in a fury, is breaking a post out of the fence and growling: 'I'll teach you to mind your tongue, you Smolensk swine!'

'The women all laugh at you, you idiots!'

Standing with difficulty, the other starts to tug an axe out of a log.

'You're maybe saying mine goes into the bushes?'

'Yours'll be the first one there!'

'Aah!' rages the first, breathing heavily with the strain as he lifts up a heavy post with vicious delight. The man from Smolensk jumps aside, but he is not quick enough and the blow lands on his shoulder.

The buffoon throws himself at the combatants.

'What are you doing, fellows? Has the devil got into you? What are you up to?'

Andrei dashes after the buffoon and flings his weight on to the post so that the peasant, breathless with fury, cannot lift it again. The buffoon is clinging to the chest of the enormous man from Smolensk, trying to keep him away from his opponent. But his feet slither apart in the greasy mud, and the Smolensk man, fiercely and purposefully brandishing the axe, slowly advances on his enemy. The peasants can no longer stand aside, and throw themselves between the two men. Realizing that he is not going to be allowed to avenge the blow to his shoulder, the Smolensk man swings the axe and lets it fly at his assailant; it misses, and the butt lands on Andrei's knee.

The buffoon flings himself at the man from Smolensk, grabs his arm and pulls him towards the barn.

'Stop it now! In the rain and all . . . Come on, mate, come on! Never mind the women. They're all the same, women are, they're all ours. You don't think they're any better in Smolensk, do you?'

'What d'you mean? Of course they're better.'

'That's fine then, if they're better. If they're better, then they're better.'

They all go back into the barn, pacifying the two who have been fighting, trying to talk them out of it.

In the meantime, at the far end of the village Kirill, standing in the mud in the middle of the street, is talking with two men on horseback. The rain makes their words inaudible.

*

16

In the barn all is peace. Some men are snoring in a corner on the hay, heavy with strong beer, others sit on the bench idly chatting and glancing at the two who have just been fighting, while these sit in opposite corners, glowering at each other.

Andrei is seated by a wall, on the floor, rubbing his bruised leg and staring out of the window into the sheets of dreary grey rain.

The buffoon gently fingers his strings, touching each one several times, and tightens the pegs.

First one string reverberates, then another, then a third . . . a beautiful, broken, monotonous sound.

Suddenly the door is thrown open with a crash, and several armed men appear in the doorway. Foremost is a huge, handsome man, broad-shouldered and red-haired, with gentle grey eyes.

There is a deathly hush. Somebody stirs in his sleep and lets out a loud moan.

Sitting on the floor, the buffoon turns his earnest, uncomprehending eyes towards the men who have just come in.

The householder is too disconcerted even to rise to his feet and greet the Prince's men; he goes on sitting on the bench, staring at his calloused hands.

The handsome leader motions the buffoon over with a nod. Laying down his psaltery, the buffoon gets up from the floor, and walks slowly towards the door, brushing wisps of straw from his knees, and smiling enquiringly at his mortal enemies.

The grey-eyed warrior takes a step forward, picks up the buffoon by the scruff of the neck with one hand, and by the seat of his pants with the other, lifts him effortlessly above his head, and slams him against the wall.

The buffoon gives a hoarse gasp as he strikes the whitewashed wall and falls down, facing the wall, his fists absurdly clenched as though he were cold. From above, pitchforks, wooden rakes and a heavy cartwheel come crashing down on top of him.

The buffoon lies there motionless. Two of the men take him by the feet and drag him outside.

The tall one glances eloquently at the man of the house, picks up the psaltery and follows his companions outside.

On the road, awash with torrential rain, stand two waggons surrounded by horsemen. In the first several men are sitting, hunched

17

up: they, too, are clearly buffoons. On the floor of the waggon lies a thin, large-headed figure, a black trickle of blood running from his mouth.

In the other waggon is a pile of confiscated musical instruments, mute, drenched in rain: psalteries, birch-bark pipes, tambourines . . .

The tall warrior throws the merry buffoon's psaltery on to the heap, and it rings out as it hits the edge of the waggon.

In the barn they are all sitting, eyes down, anxious and silent. The door creaks softly, and Kirill appears. For some moments he stares at the downcast peasants, then squats down by the door.

'Where were you?' asks Andrei after a pause.

'Outside.'

'Where?'

Kirill gives Andrei a puzzled look and repeats, 'Outside.'

'Perhaps we should be going?' suggests Daniil, frowning.

The three get up and go out on to the wet porch.

The three monks walk away from the barn, dark with rain as it recedes into the distance; they are followed by the shouting and din of the fight that has started up again with renewed violence.

The three monks make their way over fields that are desolate and swollen with water. The rain is still lashing without respite. The road has turned into a murky, rapid stream. Far ahead, through the curtain of rain, they can just make out a solitary tree.

The monks set off towards it and after a time they halt beneath a young oak with gleaming, firm leaves. At the foot of the tree it is almost dry.

'God only knows when it's going to stop,' mutters Andrei.

'Anyhow, what can you say about women,' Kirill pursues their conversation, 'they're all the same . . .'

'It seems to be getting lighter,' remarks Daniil, looking up. 'It can't go on pouring for ever.'

'All sin always has to do with them,' says Kirill in disgust; 'they're ignorant and feckless . . . And they only have the one thing in mind, only the one thing.'

'Who has only one thing in mind?' asks Daniil. 'You'd do better to leave the women alone, if that's the way you talk.'

Kirill laughs, and looks indignantly at Andrei.

'And who wouldn't then?'

'You all like talking about what you don't know. Women . . .'

'Who "all"?' says Kirill in surprise.

Daniil takes no notice of him and goes on: 'About fifteen years ago I was on my way through Moscow, and I stayed on. Some good work came my way: restoring ikons. Two ikons, old Byzantine ones. One was quite small, and the other was a big one, about like this' – he shows the size with his hands. 'And I stayed working on those ikons till the autumn. From April, that was, you see how long it took. Then just as I was ready to leave, the Tartars arrived . . . They completely surrounded the city and just stayed there. One day, two days, a week, two weeks, and showed no sign of wanting to fight. The Prince and his family had gone off to Kostroma, they said he was going to raise an army. Well, the Muscovites decided they would defend their city themselves, without the Prince. All along the walls, and by each gate, men were standing, waiting, dropping with fatigue, and the Tartars didn't make a move. You know what happens when you don't sleep for a week? You get purple and green rings in front of your eyes, you can't take anything in, you can't hear. The women and children spent twelve days shut up in the cathedral, praying to God all that time. Then the famine set in, and with it came some kind of disease: the first day you would fall ill, the next day your body would be covered with black patches, and on the third you'd be dead. Then the men raided the drink stores in their misery, and they were revelling all over Moscow. And that was the moment when the Tartars demanded payment. One hundred roubles in money and two cartloads of women's hair – from the youngest, prettiest women and girls. Two cartloads! "There you are," they said, "if you pay up we'll go, and if you don't you only have yourselves to blame."

'I can still see it now. In the fields close to the city the women and girls of Moscow were standing in a long line, moving forward between two troughs. Beside each trough there stood a Tartar with a sword, and a third Tartar stood in front of a whetstone, sharpening the swords. Hair blunts swords very quickly. The Tartars stood all around the field on their horses, and behind them stood the men, and I was among them. There the men stood, ill and weak, and watched, and I was watching too. The women walked on, and the girls, beautiful ones and plain ones, and there wasn't a single tear, as if they had turned to stone. And there, before the whole world, one after the other they took the kerchiefs from their heads, paying with their degradation for their men and for Moscow. They would take off their kerchiefs and bend forward, and the Tartar would take their plait in one hand and with the other would go ssswish! with his sword. And they made a great mountain of them. The women moving forward and behind them – ssswish, ssswish, the whetstone swished as the Tartar made another sword ready. And there stood their husbands and fathers and sons! They were too weak to do anything. And I stood there too and watched, and suddenly I felt as if I had to have more air, and I turned round, and then I saw him. He must have been ten years old or so, and there he was gazing all eyes at the women in their humiliation and misery. Though maybe they weren't miserable at all. Who can tell what goes on in a woman's head . . . Do you remember, Andrei?'

'What?' asked Andrei, who is deep in thought, staring into the rain.

'Do you remember "The Maidens' Field?"'

'No . . .'

'Did you ever have a wife?' asked Kirill.

'I did,' answers Daniil, 'she died, and five years after that I entered the monastery.'

'Did you love her?'

'I don't know . . . no, I can't have done . . .'

The rain is pouring relentlessly, drumming on the leaves, making bubbles pop up in the pools: monotonous and endless.

Andrei sighs, glances around and says suddenly: 'They shouldn't have killed the buffoon . . .'

And again the three are walking through the fields, meadows and spinneys. The rain has almost stopped. Everything around them is sodden, washed, quenched.

A radiant sun is shining. The earth steams, a black cloud slips away over the horizon, and a rainbow makes a gleaming, merry arc above the quiet river.

2 Youth: Winter 1401

Roof after roof covered in snow; black log walls; endless wooden fences; not a single window on to the street; strong gates with iron bolts; behind them, from time to time, the clank of a chain or a gruff angry bark. A maze of narrow lanes and alleyways. The trading district of Moscow, in winter; falling snow.

Down a winding lane a little, bandy-legged peasant is dragging a huge board for an ikon, painted with white size; he struggles and slithers on the roadway rutted by sledges. The board is twice the size of the man, and it is heavy and awkward to carry.

A strapping, solidly built fellow strides alongside him, offering advice.

'You know why it's hard? It's because you're bad-tempered and sulky, that's why it's hard and that's why you're getting tired so quickly.'

The little man does not answer; he is concentrating on the ground in front of his feet and breathing heavily.

'Stop sulking and losing your temper, and then it'll be easy to carry. Just try!'

The little one slips on the snow and almost falls. He only just manages to regain his balance.

'Why d'you think I'm so healthy?' the big one goes on, didactically, 'because I'm cheerful, that's why, I never let anything get me down.'

'And that's why you're so rich too, is it?' the small man's voice, muffled and angry, comes up from under the board.

'Rich? Me? Eh? What d'you mean – rich?' The irony is lost on the strapping man. 'Why don't you answer?'

They emerge on to the crossing point of two lanes, and the little man puts the board down on the snow, straightens himself painfully, and says breathlessly, 'Now you can take it as far as Zachatevka. I wasn't saying anything because that board is heavy, that's why.'

The big chap effortlessly loads the board on to his back and says: 'What d'you mean, heavy? That's no weight.'

'But I'm not strong.'

The big man livens up.

'And why aren't you strong? Because you're forever sulking and losing your temper.'

As they go off towards Zachatevka, Andrei, Kirill and Daniil, dressed for winter in battered sheepskin boots and cloth cassocks, come out of the other alleyway on to the crossroads.

'I'm blowed if I know, they're doing so much new building . . . I've no idea,' mutters Daniil as he looks around.

'Can you tell us how to get to the Cathedral of the Ascension?' Andrei asks a young woman struggling with a frozen tub beside the well.

'You can go that way,' she says, indicating the road taken by the two men with the board, 'or else that way.'

The monks choose the second route, and find themselves again in a labyrinth of snow-covered alleys squeezed between black palisades.

'Does he talk Russian?' asks Kirill suddenly, 'or just . . .'

No one answers.

'Does Theophanes the Greek talk Russian?' persists Kirill.

'I don't know,' replies Daniil. 'He must do, though, he's been living in Russia for about twenty years. Why wouldn't he talk Russian?'

Andrei and Kirill walk quickly along the alley, and Daniil finds it hard to keep up with them.

'What's he like – the Greek?' asks Andrei.

'There's lots of things said about him,' says Daniil as he tries to catch up with his companions. 'How can you tell until you've seen him yourself? Look, you two, stop going so fast, I can't run like that . . .'

'They say he's small, with a nose – like that! Hunchbacked and bad-tempered, terrible,' says Kirill.

'Aha . . .' Andrei goes on in a serious voice, 'only one leg and no arms.'

'No, come on, it's just what I was told.'

'It's cold,' remarks Andrei, clapping his face with his palm. 'My lips feel as if they were made of wood.'

The monks walk over a crossroads and vanish round a corner.

The two men with the board reappear out of the next alleyway. The big one is carrying the board, the small man walking alongside him.

'Is it heavy?' asks the latter.

'Leave me be.'

'It's surely heavy, isn't it?'

The big man slips on an icy turning and leans up against the fence.

'It's the last time I work with you,' he utters between his teeth.

'Hey, friend, carry this board up for us! My man here is worn out!' the small peasant shouts after a sleigh, drawn by a sweating mare, as it goes past.

'You know where you can go,' snarls the big chap, pushing himself off the supportive fence with some difficulty, and making his way to the middle of the street.

The two turn down the next alley.

The three monks come out on to the crossroads.

'I just don't see how he can do it in front of everyone,' says Andrei, wondering.

'Why should it worry him?' Daniil laughs. 'He's not a thief, he's not a crook.'

They are all in high good spirits.

'We're not crooks either, but I wouldn't be able to paint anything with people looking on,' says Kirill.

'No, of course we're not thieves either,' Daniil agrees.

'What if they don't let us in?' Andrei smiles.

'Why, they'll surely let us in!' says Daniil in surprise. 'They say the people come in, and there he is, painting, and people watch. And he paints fast, they say. Finished works. In Novgorod an old woman came in the morning when they had just brought him a board. And by the evening there was the finished ikon. Everyone went away, and she stayed on. She went on standing there, went on looking and looking, and then she died.'

'What of?' Kirill is astonished.

'From fear, that's what it was . . .'

'Why fear?'

'Well, she was scared and she died.'

Andrei looks at Daniil, puzzled. 'Well . . .'

'There's the cathedral.' Kirill stops in the middle of the alley. 'Look, there it is!'

*

An excited crowd is milling around in front of the cathedral. The two peasants – the little one and the strapping one – are struggling in the doorway, trying to push the huge board through the narrow opening. They try first one way and then another, leaning the board over or laying it flat. It will not go through. Despite the frost, the men are drenched in sweat, and panting, as they shuffle their feet about in the porch; and the wooden board clonks against the rough, gritty stone of the cathedral, over which an icy wind blows freshly fallen snow.

The crowd are restive.

'Why aren't they letting us in?'

A Brother who is fussing around the men with the board turns in alarm and shouts at the crowd: 'Can't you use your heads? Theophanes only came back from Novgorod yesterday, and you go, "they're not letting us in"! The orders are that no one is to be allowed in today!'

'Only just back, and straight away they shut us out!' snarls someone in the crowd.

'We'd make holes in his board by looking at it then, would we?' says a tall, thin old man, throwing a sardonic glance at the Brother. 'That Greek of yours is getting too full of himself, that's for sure,' he declares categorically, and turns away in contempt. He does not walk away, however, for he still hopes he might be allowed in.

Some visiting monk tries to reason with the flustered Brother: 'Just let me in by myself, I'll stand there quietly and watch, no one will notice. Then afterwards I'll . . .' And the monk makes a vague gesture which the well-trained Brother immediately recognizes as a promise to make it worth his while.

'Later . . .' adds the monk.

The peasants push with all their strength against the great, bulky board which protrudes from the black cavity of the doorway, and, as a stone, dislodged from the lintel comes tumbling down, the peasants and the board disappear inside the cathedral. The Brother trots after them. A heavy bolt crashes home.

'So much for watching him,' mutters Andrei, wrapping his worn cassock around him and jumping up and down to try and warm up.

'I told you they wouldn't let us in.' Kirill grins.

'Let's wait a little.' Daniil tries to keep his spirits up. 'They may still let us in.'

'Oh! Come on!' Andrei makes a dismissive gesture. 'Let's go, what's the point . . .'

At that moment the door opens with a clang, and the peasants, worn out but satisfied, hiding their wages inside their shirtfronts, appear in the doorway. They are followed by the Brother, who emerges frowning painfully, looks at the crowd and announces in a husky voice: 'It's no good your standing there, can't you understand? My orders are not to let anyone in. Those are my orders, do you hear?'

'Wait a minute, now!' mutters Daniil, starting to elbow his way through the crowd towards the cathedral entrance. Andrei and Kirill, trying not to look hopeful, watch their companion's stratagem.

'Listen, dear friend,' Daniil addresses the Brother, tugging at his sleeve, 'we're from the Andronnikov Monastery. We've come to look at the beautiful things you have here, at your Theophanes. And there's a pair of young ones with me; they're ikon painters, too, apprentices. Maybe you could let us in, eh?'

'But my orders . . . Why ask me, I'm not in charge! Those are my orders.'

'Come, who's in charge if it isn't you! We've been walking since morning, we're frozen, all we want is to see the Greek, to look at his work. Eh?' Daniil stealthily slips a silver coin into the Brother's palm. 'It's not just for fun, it's our work, don't you see. And I've got young Andrei and Kirill with me.'

Without looking at Daniil, and hesitating for the sake of propriety, the Brother takes hold of the door handle.

'I'll go and ask . . . Maybe you'll be lucky, I don't know . . .'

The spry little monk who has been hovering around the entrance all this time comes hurrying up to Daniil: 'Would you take me in with you? Eh? If they let you in. Will you take me too?'

After a few moments the Brother thrusts his head through the door and looks severely at Daniil.

'Anyone here from Andronnikov? – come in!'

Daniil waves. Andrei and Kirill push their way through the indignant crowd.

'They are colleagues, colleagues!' explains the Brother in businesslike tones as he watches the monks approach. 'Painters . . . Nobody else!'

With remarkable adroitness the persistent little monk manages to reach the door before anyone else, and, gazing into the Brother's eyes with doglike devotion, he repeats like an incantation: 'I'm with them, I'm with them.'

All four disappear behind the door. For some time the iron ring of the handle goes on swinging to and fro, squeaking and knocking. The people left standing outside, sad and offended, watch it, and listen to the footsteps as they die away.

Through a dark ante-chapel they enter the cathedral and stop on the threshold. There is nobody there.

The dim light that filters through the high windows, long and narrow as loopholes, falls gently over the upper part of the white-washed walls.

The Brother slams the door and goes off up a dark staircase.

'Where is he?' asks Kirill.

'There's no one here . . .' says Daniil quietly.

'Can't see anything . . .' Andrei sounds bewildered.

'Hush, you two,' Daniil hisses at his companions.

Their voices are thrown back, muffled and hollow, by the twilit walls.

'It's so spacious!' says Andrei in amazement.

Slowly, allowing his eyes to become used to the darkness, he walks across the echoing flagstones till he comes to the far wall, which stands bathed in greyish light.

'O-oh . . . Think of painting a great cathedral like that . . . Eh, Andrei?' Daniil's voice is at once joyful and sad.

Andrei is standing motionless as a statue by the opposite wall.

'It would take a year, or even more,' adds Kirill, vaguely.

The stray monk is twisting his head this way and that like a bird and staring anxiously into the darkness of the corners.

'What about Byzantium, working there . . .' Daniil goes on. 'No frosts, or anything . . . You could start in January.'

Andrei, not moving a muscle, his eyebrows raised in astonishment, is standing in a corner and gazing at an enormous ikon propped up against the wall.

'You mean there's no snow there either?' asks the little monk, looking round in alarm.

'Where?' asks Daniil.

26

'Out there, in Byzantium . . .'

'None. Only rain. And not much of that.'

'It's a bit dark here though. Eh, Daniil?' murmurs Kirill softly.

'Why have a lot of light? It's exactly right. Andrei, what are you up to?'

Andrei does not answer. He is standing transfixed in front of the ikon, his lips moving helplessly.

'Andrei!'

'Come here . . .' Andrei calls out in a whisper, his eyes still on the board.

'What?' Daniil does not understand.

'Come over here,' repeats Andrei, irritated, but his voice is still quiet.

'Perhaps we should call somebody? Eh?' Kirill is losing patience. 'Where have they all vanished to?'

'Come here!' Andrei suddenly shouts at the top of his voice.

They all dash over to him, realizing from his tone that something has happened.'

And they stop, stunned.

They stand in silence in front of Theophanes's ikon.

Andrei gazes at it, concentrating, almost angry, holding the palm of his hand over his nose and mouth.

Daniil, eyebrows raised, smiles in surprise, kindly and bewildered.

Kirill stands half-facing the ikon, his face barely discernable in the darkness . . .

The little monk keeps crossing himself with small, rapid gestures and glancing anxiously at the others.

Their thoughts ring out simultaneously, the discordant notes of their souls sounding in an agitated trio.

ANDREI: Those pupils are so full of light, so full of light . . . And I might have lived my life through and never seen it. Or even heard of it. How can it be that this was made by some wretched, mortal human being? (*Pause.*)

And the way he stares. Excited, and angry. How long does a man have to study to be able to paint like that? Or maybe you don't have to study at all? I shall come to him tomorrow and fall at his feet and ask to be his apprentice, to wash his brushes . . .

DANIIL: Just look at that texture! Like sparks flying! He's not afraid of anything. And what could he be afraid of, being able to paint like that? What a talent, what a great talent. The longer you look the more frightening it is. But what is there to be afraid of? Really? Don't I know everything about myself already. (*He laughs.*) Or maybe there's still something I don't know? Oh, Daniil, Daniil! (*He laughs.*)

KIRILL: (*Shouting*) I don't know how to do anything! I can't do anything! I can't see anything! I can't feel line! I can't feel colour! I am simply blind! (*Calmly.*) No, it was just that there was nobody to teach me. If only I were a lad now, like Andrei. Tomorrow I shall try and paint a new ikon – like that.

Stunned, the monks stand in the shadows of the cathedral.

The frightened little monk suddenly starts to recite in a low voice: 'Mother of God, holy Virgin, hail, blessed Mary . . .'

The adolescent's tremulous prayer resounds within the empty walls.

A low side door cautiously creaks open, and the small, frail, dark figure of an old man emerges. He observes the monks, smiles, and comes creeping stealthily along the wall. A few paces away from them he stops, listening to the little monk's 'Mother of God', then he fills his lungs with air and lets out a strident yell: 'Aaah!'

Terrified, the painters spin round. The little monk, panic-stricken, leaps up from his knees, trips over the hem of his cassock and falls down, barely aware of what is happening.

When eventually, after several convulsive efforts, he manages to stand up, he sees Theophanes the Greek roaring with laughter in front of him – scraggy, hair on end, eagle-nosed, and with one solitary tooth.

'Ikon painters, are you?' he asks, laughing helplessly. 'They told me.' He suddenly becomes serious. 'Come to have a look?'

'That's it,' answers Daniil quietly, looking closely at Theophanes.

'Go on, then, you look. I'll be putting on drying oil presently.'

He goes up to the ikon, stares at it with a proprietary squint, and delicately removes a speck of dust from its gleaming surface.

The monks gaze at the ikon and Theophanes directs a sidelong stare at them.

Andrei looks at the Greek in surprise.

'Why are you looking at me, that's where you should be looking,' says Theophanes to Andrei.

'They say you paint very fast?' asks Andrei.

They all turn silently to look at Theophanes.

'I do. Why? It's the only way I can. I get fed up otherwise. Once I was sweating away for a whole week. I gave up on it, I'd had enough.'

'You threw it away?' asks Kirill.

'In fact I've had enough altogether – up to here!' sighs Theophanes, and draws his hand across his throat. 'I shall die soon,' he adds, coughing.

'You shouldn't say that . . .' says Daniil, uncertainly.

'Why not,' Theophanes continues. 'I am going to die. Two nights ago I dreamt that an angel was saying, "Come along with me," he said. So I said, "I'll be dying soon enough anyway, without you." . . . So . . .'

'What about that ikon you didn't finish, where did you put it? Did you throw it out?' asks Kirill.

'No, why would I throw it out?' Theophanes sighs. 'I used it for pressing pickled cabbage.'

'We were told that you paint with everyone looking on?' says Daniil.

'Why not? Let them watch if they enjoy it.'

'But why aren't they being allowed in today?'

'I'd let them in myself, only the Grand Prince is supposed to be coming in today to have a look. I don't mind. Only when the Grand Prince comes no one is allowed in.'

The Greek sighs again, looks up at the bright slits of windows and, slapping the rough stuccoed wall with his palm, says wistfully, 'It's very light here. And cramped. That's the trouble . . .'

Andrei, Daniil and Kirill are wandering about on the foundations of the Cathedral of the Annunciation, where building work has already started; snow lies on the ground. It is dusk. Near by, a drip of water, colder with the evening, makes a steady plopping sound.

'Haven't we hung around here long enough? Let's go . . .' says Kirill.

'What a cathedral that's going to be. Beautiful!' Daniil is gazing around.

From one low foundation wall to the other black planks are laid criss-cross, covered with clean, densely packed snow that has thawed a little, and gleams.

'Are the days growing any longer?' asks Andrei.

'Not yet,' replies Daniil, glancing to either side.

'I've had enough of winter.' Andrei hunches his shoulders.

'You're always like that,' grumbles Kirill, 'first one thing then the other.'

'What?' asks Andrei.

'You said yourself you couldn't live without winter,' Kirill goes on.

'I'm fed up with the slush, not with winter.'

'It's a weird sort of winter,' says Daniil, 'every week there's a thaw.'

'Soon there won't be any winter or any summer,' says Kirill bitterly, 'it'll just be one endless thaw.'

'I wonder who's going to paint it?' asks Andrei suddenly, banging his fist on the frosty stone of the foundations.

No one speaks. Moscow is quiet. All that can be heard is the plash of the drip, growing gradually slower as it freezes, and, from the other side of the black fence, the algid yelp of a watch dog.

'Can you imagine painting something as colossal as that?' wonders Daniil thoughtfully.

Then, glancing at his crestfallen companions, he suggests cheerfully: 'Come, let's go, it's late.'

None of them moves.

'It's too dark to go home,' says Andrei, 'we must find ourselves a place to spend the night in Moscow.'

'How long will it stand there?' wonders Kirill. 'Five hundred years?'

No one answers.

'Does Theophanes have many pupils?' Andrei turns to Daniil.

'I don't know,' replies Daniil, 'he probably does.'

'I think it would be very difficult working with him, you know,' remarks Kirill.

'I'd like something to eat.' Andrei yawns.

Daniil suddenly remembers: 'Brothers, I think we left the bundle of food there.'

'No, we didn't.' Kirill goes over to a pile of shavings powdered with snow. 'I put it down somewhere here.'

Andrei aimlessly kicks a huge white stone out of the heap of hewn limestone. Deep in thought he picks it up, tenses himself, and lifts it above his head.

'You're tough, aren't you!' calls Kirill from a little way off. 'One wouldn't think it, to look at you. What you should be doing is humping stones around, not painting ikons.'

'What power!' sighs Andrei quietly, and throws the stone to the ground with all his might.

'What?' Daniil asks, standing a short distance away.

'Theophanes has power.'

'What?' asks Kirill as he picks the bundle up off the ground.

'Theophanes has a gift from God,' explains Daniil.

Andrei climbs up, level with the highest point of the foundations. He gazes around.

Dusk is falling. Two peasants are walking down a nearby street. One is carrying a huge board for an ikon. They turn down an alleyway and head towards the cathedral square.

'What are we hanging around here for,' mutters Andrei, shivering. 'Come on.'

No one moves, it is as if they have not heard.

Andrei stamps his feet on the scaffolding on which he is standing.

All the snow falls off the boards at once, laying bare the black, insubstantial skeleton of the scaffolding.

Evening is drawing on. The murky red sun is growing colder in the frosty air. The pine forest is as still as if it were made of wrought iron, transfixed, resonant; and the heavy snow of several weeks lies sleeping on the dark, springy, green needles.

Figures in black cassocks move about the dry undergrowth carpeting the ground: monks of the Andronnikov Monastery. Axes thud, and frost dust, thrown up by tremulously dying trees, scatters and sparkles in the coppery evening light.

Near by, swinging their axes in turn and exhaling strenuously at each stroke, Andrei and Kirill are felling a pine tree. Yellow pine chips go flying into the snow.

The monks wield their heavy axes without speaking. Sweat is pouring down their faces and stinging their eyes, and they screw up their faces as if they were working in smoke; they are out of breath.

Suddenly Kirill straightens his back, throws his axe down on to the snow, breathes out, and starts to feel his stomach, staring fixedly as if he is listening.

'Something hurting . . . What's going on here, eh? My stomach, is it?'

'You've eaten something,' says Andrei, going on working.

'Are you all right?' asks Kirill, with a grimace of pain, still feeling his stomach.

'Yes, I think so . . .'

'I've never had any pain before either, but now there's something . . .'

'Sit down for a bit,' suggests Andrei, 'maybe it'll pass.'

'Oh, never mind.' Kirill waves his hand dismissively and, picking up his axe, resumes work.

'Never mind, it'll pass,' Andrei reassures him.

They work on for a time in silence.

'If you start having stomach-ache as well,' says Kirill, 'it'll mean we were poisoned together. We ate something foul.'

'You probably had some of the fish that old man brought yesterday . . .'

Kirill gives Andrei a sharp, hostile look, then grins and raises his axe.

'You know, when I look at you all I just don't understand . . .' he goes on, turning away. 'You're hard, somehow. Cruel . . . Although maybe that's the way it has to be, I don't know . . .'

'Who do you mean by "you all"?' asks Andrei thoughtfully.

'You, the young.'

'What are you driving at?'

'Nothing, I'm just saying. There's only seven years between us and everything has changed. You'll insult a person, even an old man – and you won't even notice. And the other young monks too, you're all the same. We lived in a different time. You've had it easy.'

'You're being very complicated somehow . . .' Andrei looks remote, he has not been paying attention for some time and is thinking about something completely different.

'Last night I dreamt about my mother.'

'Wait, about your mother,' Kirill is agitated and worried, 'and I'm not being complicated. Look, tell me honestly, before God . . .'

But Andrei is not listening, his heart is tightening with a

mysterious sense of something about to happen, something he has long been waiting for, and that rouses fear and hope in him at the same time. His memory frees itself of the present, and through it, to the half-heard sound of axes in the pine wood, there move naked and painfully acute moments from his past . . .

There was Andrei – a lad – jumping into a cold, clear lake; hazy pillars slanted down to touch the ghostly bed and lit up quivering, almost pulsating, algae; a startled crucian carp darted away, its gold scales dimly gleaming; a pure, sandy bank rose slowly and brightly from the depths, glistening, rippling with sunlight and water and grey shadows; the long, solitary trail of a bivalve was suddenly intersected by another, identical to it, and then stretched on into the shining warmth of the sun, to the spot where the sand bank almost touched the trembling surface of the lake (like liquid glass) towards which Andrei was swimming, eyes open under the water, arms stretched out, and where he caught up with it, carefully picked it out of the sand and held it up to his eyes to watch it hide its tender, defenceless body between its ugly, convulsively clenched shutters.

Then he remembers what Daniil had recalled as the three of them were standing under the oak tree in the rain: women moving over a field in a long, terrible line – all different, beautiful and ugly, some no more than little girls, with lips swollen from fruitless, salt tears that came from the very depths of their souls, others no longer young, their gaze firm and full of hatred; they walked slowly, solemnly, as if playing some absurd game; bonded by their own silence and the expectation of a real, very painful death, one by one taking off their kerchiefs, abstracted, looking ahead shamelessly and obstinately, following one another too slowly for an onlooker to hope that all might be well in the end, because close by sat a Tartar by a block of wood, chopping off the women's plaits.

Then he was flying downhill on a toboggan, his eyes watering in the wind and the glistening snow flashing past, surrounded with a sparkling cloud of diamond dust. The whole slope was covered with the black figures of boys and girls. Black trees went floating past from right to left and left to right and at the same time were rushing towards him. And behind them was the winter river, a white sheet with a track cutting across its dazzling surface and black holes gaping in the ice. Beside these women knelt and rinsed their washing. At the bottom, where he skidded to a halt in the middle of the river and was showered with dusty snow, a heap of children. And a shaggy dog, covered with burdock, leapt barking on to his chest or tried to lick the flushed, laughing face of a little girl who had managed to extricate herself form beneath the game of 'sacks on the mill' that the boys had set up on the creaking ice, in the very middle of the river.

And once again in his memory there rose the wide field over which they made their way barefoot through soft, deep dust which grew warmer as the day wore on; the women's and girls' plaits swung as they walked, slithering to right and left beside their hanging arms; tightly clutched in their hands were clean kerchiefs, the ends dragged on the road which they had to cross before they reached the waggon; there, with his back to them, sat a sweating shaven-headed Tartar; his arm was numb with fatigue, he was swinging it mechanically, striking blow after blow with a sabre that flashed in the sun.

Under the water again: all at once, as if a single thread held them together, a line of tiny, startled fish made a burst of silvery sparks; the opaque, cold depths of the lake was resistant, pushing him upwards, his hair crept into his eyes and floated above his head; a slippery, dark-red water-lily stalk, covered in minute bubbles that gleamed like quicksilver, was swaying before him, and Andrei pulled the flower up to his face and for some time examined the opaque, sunlit, yellow halo it made under the water, but it was smooth to the touch, and it floated slowly up to the surface when Andrei decided to let it go; through the water he could see the sun rocking, swaying to and fro, hazy and gleaming; then, pushing himself off from the resilient water with his hands, he began to go towards it, scared that he would not have enough air, would asphyxiate, that his lungs might burst – and at that moment some-one's heavy shadow fell on to the water, sharp rays spread out around it, and at once the water became cold and terrifying, there was a surge, and a resounding clap, and a man fell in from the bank, his coarse shirt rapidly turned black in the water, his dead eyes were wide open, and blood was curling like smoke on the current. Andrei rushed through it, his mouth convulsively opened, until he drew a mouthful of life-giving, warm air redolent of marshland.

The man had been killed with an arrow.

From somewhere far away Andrei catches the menacing creak of a tree, a hollow sound, at the utmost point of strain.

'Let go, I'll knock it away!' comes Kirill's voice.

'Move! Get away!' yells Kirill. 'Watch out! Are you crazy! Andrei!'

Andrei hears a rat-a-tat that gradually swells to a roar.

The ancient tree falls with an ominous crash, breaking branches, scattering black needles and raising a cloud of snow-dust.

Andrei, pushed away from the falling tree by Kirill, stands gazing into the distance, fiddling thoughtfully with the rope around his waist.

Kirill is flabbergasted. 'Well – Brother!'

The cloud of snow slowly settles.

Andrei turns and walks away, oblivious of everything, beside the fallen tree trunk, stumbling through the snow and stepping over branches.

'What are you doing, Andrei?' Kirill shouts after him.

Andrei does not answer.

'Andrei!'

'I can do better . . .'

'Better than what?'

'Better . . .'

'Better than whom?'

'Than the Greek. Than Theophanes.'

'Have you no fear of God, Andrei? That's a sin. That's pride . . .'

'Lord . . .' Andrei sighs and covers his face with his hands.

Kirill stares after him, nonplussed, still holding his axe.

Andrei smiles and walks further and further into the virgin snow.

He comes out on to the main road leading up to the monastery and stops on the verge: a huge, weary herd of horses is moving past him along the road, enveloped in warm, breathy steam.

A number of horsemen, Tartar drivers, ride behind them.

Andrei stops, and for a long time gazes steadily at the horses as they go past. They are shaking their heads wearily and snorting; glistening pieces of ice have frozen into thin, spiky beards; drearily they churn up the yellow snow on the road, chinking with their bits, their wet, steaming flanks twitching; their soft, velvety lips hang mournfully, and they stare thoughtfully, with sad, mauve eyes, at the useless, inexplicable objects moving past them.

Andrei watches the horses' sloping, soft backs as they move forward in a dense mass, trying to warm themselves by staying closely packed, not looking at one another, in a half-waking state induced by the arduous, never-ending road; occasionally one of them gives a frantic swish of its muddy tail, or stops, throwing back its head and rolling its eyes, making way for a mare that unexpectedly crosses its path.

Andrei gazes absently, already thinking about something quite other than the road, or the horses, or even the winter.

'Get up, you can ride,' a voice interrupts his reflections.

Andrei looks up and sees a wealthily dressed Tartar mounted on a foaming stallion. The Tartar is smiling, his whole face gathered in wrinkles, as he restrains the handsome animal dancing under him.

'Thanks, I'll walk,' answers Andrei, and he turns and continues on his way along the edge of the road.

The Tartar shakes his reins and rides after him.

For a while he follows Andrei, who can feel the horseman's mocking gaze on the back of his head. Then the Tartar catches up with him, and rides beside him in silence, touching his elbow with his foot in the stirrup.

Andrei walks on, not lifting his head and trying not to take any notice of him.

'You're tired, up you get,' Andrei hears a smiling invitation.

Quickening his pace he tries to overtake the unhurried rider. The Tartar, observing his manoeuvre, proceeds to edge the monk off the verge and into the deep, untrodden snow.

Andrei resists, surreptitiously and obstinately. Then the stirrup digs painfully into his elbow. Andrei goes tumbling into the snow, comes to a stop and, giving up the pointless battle, he looks up at the smiling Tartar with a look full of sober hatred.

'Get up, you can ride,' repeats the Tartar.

Andrei lowers his eyes, wavers for a moment, then, making up his mind, walks around the trader, untwists the reins of the saddled grey mare tethered to the Tartar's stirrup, and heaves himself into the saddle.

For a time they ride slowly, abreast.

'How about my horses, then?' asks the Tartar suddenly.

'I don't know anything about them . . .'

'What, nothing at all? . . . Well, why don't you answer?'

Andrei does not reply. The Tartar stares into his face, enjoying his discomfiture.

Andrei turns away, biting his lip, and looks at the snow-covered evening fields, the oily white willows beside the road, the forest, blue on the horizon.

'You for Moscow?' the Tartar addresses Andrei again.

'I'm not going far. The Andronnikov Monastery.'

'Tartar horses – good horses.' He must be very anxious to talk after his long, lonely journey.

Andrei says nothing, and his fingers, blue with cold, keep tying and untying the knot in the leather bridle.

'Your earth is good earth. Rich. In Moscow I sell my horse well,' the Tartar goes on. 'What do you think?'

'I don't know . . . Most likely you will.'

'Tartar horses are strong horses, tasty horses,' says the Tartar and, making a smacking sound with his tongue, he starts to sing in a husky, powerful voice.

Andrei, swaying in the worn but clearly expensive saddle, looks at the mare's tough, grey withers, the muddy, trampled road the colour of beer, dotted with apple-sized lumps of horsedung, and cannot make out whether the Tartar's song is sad or merry – his voice is broken and throaty, his slanting eyes half-closed, and he sways nonchalantly in rhythm with the stallion's walk.

Moving past them are fields, lying desolate under the snow, broken fences, solitary, bedraggled trees with empty winter nests.

Just as Andrei decides to dismount, and swings his leg over the pommel, the Tartar breaks off his song and, seizing him by the elbow, hisses between his teeth, without looking him in the eyes: 'You sit, sit.'

And they go on again in silence, gently rocking as if in a boat.

37

Andrei sits with the reins loose, his frozen hands tucked under his armpits, angrily staring ahead.

'Cold?' enquires the Tartar suddenly.

'No,' says Andrei, and picks up the reins.

'Why you lie?' The Tartar takes his silver-embroidered, fur-trimmed mittens from his hands and proffers them to Andrei. 'Here!'

'I don't need them.'

'Take them, I got them off a dead Russian prince. Take them.'

'I'm warm enough.'

'You joke. Take them.'

Andrei shakes his head without looking at the Tartar.

'Take them!' yells the Tartar in a burst of indignation.

'Get away! Leave off!' Andrei shouts, furiously.

Unexpectedly, the Tartar laughs, puts the mittens on his pommel, unties his saddle-bag, pulls out a bundle, unrolls a thin piece of felt and takes out a lump of dried meat. Then he takes an expensive knife with a silver handle from inside his coat, cuts off a thin slice of meat and puts it into his cheek to thaw.

'Want some horse meat?' he says thickly.

'No.'

'You not like it?'

'No, I don't.'

'Never mind, you get used to it.'

The monastery walls rise spectrelike in the frosty evening air.

The stallion suddenly stumbles under the Tartar and slips, its feet drumming rapidly on the ground, and it breaks into a trot. Only just managing not to lose the mittens, the meat and the dagger, the merchant swears in Tartar and checks the stallion with his whip.

'I have four Russian wives,' he declares, smacking his lips with relish, 'three good, other bad.'

Slowly wiping his mouth with his sleeve, the Tartar suddenly stops chewing and looks hard at Andrei. Then, without hurrying, he tucks the bundle of meat and the knife into his coat, and all of a sudden shouts in a strident, vicious voice: 'Go on then, walk!'

The monk turns, taken aback, and looks at the Tartar.

'Get you off my mangy, stinking, cursed Tartar horse!'

Andrei throws down the reins and jumps down on to the road;

he hurries off without looking round, his lips angrily pursed and his hands folded on his stomach.

The Tartar rides a few yards behind him, staring at the monk's back and saying nothing. Finally, with a crooked smile, he says dejectedly: 'All your life you be on your feet.'

It is difficult to walk along the edge of the road: his feet keep slipping down into the snow that has built up against the ridges and is melting.

The wooden walls of the monastery move past him majestically.

The Tartar impassively dogs his steps.

'I saw your prince myself, he came to the Settlement, fell off his horse, crawled on his knees, tore his whole kaftan,' concludes the horseman in his husky voice, and utters a thin, unpleasant laugh.

Andrei stops abruptly, white as the snow, and says softly: 'I shall kill you!' – and he picks up a frozen beam from the road, swings it over his head, and throws it at the rider. The latter ducks with the adroit, unhurried movement of the experienced fighter, and the heavy post, after slipping from Andrei's wooden hands, strikes the stallion on the crupper. The horse neighs, goes down on its haunches, and gives a sideways jump, but the rider effortlessly keeps his seat, and glancing over his shoulder calls back in a quiet, resentful tone: 'You wicked. All Russians wicked.' He touches the stallion's wet flanks with his heels and goes off slowly after the herd.

'But I give you a gift for your wickedness . . .' The Tartar thrusts four fingers into his mouth, and a throbbing, brigand's whistle rings out over the darkening countryside.

The stallion carries the Tartar off in the tracks of the herd, and the thin, wiry mare, obedient to the Tartar's command, stays there on the road. She stands next to Andrei, blowing out her nostrils, her flanks quivering. The wind plays in her mane and in her tangled tail. She shifts her weight from hoof to hoof and stares at Andrei.

The herd of horses vanish round a bend. Andrei begins to back slowly towards the monastery gates. The mare snorts, loudly and anxiously as if afraid her new master might leave her there for ever, and takes a few steps towards the gates.

The monk squeezes through a narrow gap in the gate, slips on the snow, and hurriedly, without looking back, goes off across the empty yard in the direction of the cells.

The black mare goes up to the gates, sniffs at a crack in the planks, snorts again, and utters a long, plaintive whinny as she watches him walk away, his figure melting into the gathering dusk.

3   The Hunt: Summer 1403

Two figures are walking deep in the forest, along a track overgrown with bushy aspen: Andrei and his pupil Foma, a lanky boy of about fifteen.

It is early on a summer morning, and steam rises above the tall grass and the clumps of Ivan-and-Marya*: the earth is warming up, recovering in the sunshine from the cold rain of the night.

Andrei walks ahead, while Foma dawdles along behind him, staring drearily in front of his feet and from time to time fingering his shoulder and face, swollen from bee stings.

'Always shoving his nose into what doesn't concern him!' Andrei's voice is indignant.

'What do you mean, doesn't concern? What am I . . .'

'Who asked you? Did I ask you? Or did Father Daniil ask you?'

'Maybe he did,' mutters Foma grimly.

Andrei is so taken aback that he stops in his tracks.

'When?'

'Well, he would've, you never manage to get everything done . . .' grumbles Foma.

'You've ruined a good ikon.'

'You said yourself it was "not a bad little ikon",' Foma justifies himself.

'Whatever it was like, by your standards it was good! Some craftsman, self-taught, sat and worked at it . . . It must be a hundred years old, at least. And you just took it into your head without asking anybody, and slapped on some blue . . . D'you imagine an ikon can be restored just like that? People like you are two a penny. Anyone can chuck paint on.'

'I'll paint another one on it.'

Andrei stops, swipes at a white, roadside cow parsley with the flat of his hand, and speaks fast, angrily: 'You listen to me: if you want to learn, learn, but if you don't, then go away, the sooner the

*melampyrum nemorosum – Translator

41

better, and try . . .' Andrei breaks off. 'I spent three years cleaning Daniil's brushes for him before – miraculously – he let me touch an ikon. And then it wasn't to restore it, only to clean it.'

'But you won't let me touch one?' Foma sounds like an adult.

'How could I let you? You lie as you breathe. Look at how you appeared yesterday, and the state your cassock was in, all sticky. Where had you really been?'

'In the apiary!' answers Foma, with challenging candour.

'And yesterday you said you'd been swimming. Look at you now!' – Andrei pauses beside a great forest dew-pond, full of succulent marsh grass and enormous, dazzling buttercups. The water is clear and slightly yellowish. 'Just look at you.' Andrei gives Foma a push on the back of the head. 'Why don't you put some water over it at least, or rub it with earth, otherwise you're going to swell up like a hog . . .'

'Must be too late now,' Foma mutters, 'it won't help.'

'You're forever making things up, Brother.' Andrei gazes thoughtfully into the water.

A water-boatman skims rapidly and smoothly over the water, pushing itself off from the springy surface with sudden, abrupt movements.

'I'm even wondering if you haven't caught some illness?'

The water-spider takes a few little strokes, stops, and freezes. It is slowly carried along by the forest breeze . . .

'Eh? What illness?' asks Foma in alarm.

'There must be some illness that makes a person lie so that he can't stop.'

'Well . . . Everybody lies.' Foma takes a lump of wet clay from the bottom of the puddle and puts it against his swollen face. 'You call the Father Superior every name under the sun amongst yourselves, and then you kiss his hand . . . Brother Nicholas got himself dead drunk and pretended he was ill . . . And you yourself . . .'

'What about me?' Andrei snaps.

'Oh, nothing.' Foma stands up.

A wagtail alights on the damp grey sand. It runs along on its black, wiry legs, leaving barely perceptible tracks, then suddenly stops to watch something moving, probably a water-boatman, and waggles its busy tail in tiny, rapid, springy movements . . .

*

Beside a tree, in the shade of some bushes covered in nondescript flowers, around which forest flies and wasps are buzzing in the warm sunshine, stands Kirill. He is stripping the bark off the long, uneven trunk of a young hazel sapling, and listening with a smile to the conversation between teacher and pupil.

'Well, go on? M'm?' Andrei urges him crossly.

'You don't always tell the truth yourself!' Foma bursts out. 'If you don't like a person, then you'll never tell him the truth to his face, not for anything, you won't, d'you think I'm such a fool I don't see?'

'Who is it I don't like?' Andrei is taken aback.

Kirill sighs, smiling, and leans his back against the tree.

'Have you gone quite daft, then? Don't you understand anything? . . .'

Insulted, Foma gives a portentous smirk and goes on rubbing wet clay over his face.

Now there are two water-boatmen running across the deep water, pushing themselves in turn with supple, thin legs that fold in two. They run, skirting around pine needles and blades of grass with silver bubbles of air clinging to them, and then freeze in mid-course, and the breeze blows them stubbornly across the puddle, in which the tops of the trees lie mirrored. The wagtail hops about on the edge, tracking down spiders, bobbing her heavy tail and twitching her little head. Then she hops right up to the puddle, and her head twitches as she watches the darting water-boatmen. Any moment now she will catch one.

'Look, Foma,' whispers Andrei.

'What?' Foma pouts sulkily.

'I said, look.'

'What at?'

The wagtail freezes for an instant, then hops away and vanishes.

'Nothing, you blockhead . . .' Andrei sighs, and walks off down the path. 'Why I took you on as an apprentice, I really don't know.'

'You always do that . . . You say something and then you say the opposite. You said yourself I can see better than any of the others.'

'Who sees better than any of the others? I said so?'

'Yes, you did.'

'What are you talking about?' says Andrei impatiently.

'When Father Daniil was asking you about the apprentices you pointed to me and said, "That one can see a yard into the ground and he likes azure." You did . . .'

'You were different then, you tried, you didn't tell fibs . . .'

'All the same I can see better than any of them!'

'What?' Andrei stops angrily in the middle of the road.

'I can . . .'

'Can you!' Andrei flares up. 'Very well! You're making a big mistake . . . You're going to be cleaning brushes for the next three years. Anything else?'

'Well . . .' says Foma uncertainly, already regretting his bravado.

'What's that?' asks Andrei, pointing at a willow growing by the road, its light branches swaying in the wind.

'What . . . A willow . . .' Foma replies slowly, scared. 'And ivy.'

Andrei smiles contemptuously.

'Ivy . . . What d'you mean, ivy! It's a hop, you scarecrow.'

'All right, hop.'

'Not all right, hop! Not all right, hop – but hop!'

'What are you shouting about?' Foma is offended. 'It was your idea, and now you're shouting.'

'Three years of cleaning brushes, lad. You're ignorant, Brother. Hop, you know . . . It's something quite special. It doesn't recognize any of the rules. Look, it's thrown this shoot off to the right, and it wanted to swing this one out to the left, but there's no room, so it made it hang down – and again it's beautiful.'

Andrei is gesturing as he expands on his theme, more and more carried away by it.

'As far as the drunken hop is concerned, rules just don't exist. Trees and grass and flowers all grow upwards, but this one, look at it, it crawled up to the top of the trunk, and when it couldn't go any further it started growing downwards. And it always looks good. It makes things beautiful in whatever way it wants. . .' Andrei breaks off, suddenly looking furious: Foma is standing with his back to him, not listening, demonstratively looking away.

'You know,' says Andrei quietly, 'you've become so clever that I am not going to teach you any more.'

'What would I be learning anyhow,' says Foma, turning away with a grin, 'if all I'm doing is cleaning brushes.'

His voice trembles with resentment. Out of the corner of his eye he watches the sinuous hop tendrils swinging in the wind.

'That's it! I've had enough. E-nough! Go and be Kirill's pupil, God forgive me.' Andrei turns and walks off angrily into the wood. Trying to appear calm, he hums under his breath.

'All right, so I'll go. What of it . . .' Foma grumbles after him. With eyes full of tears he looks closely at the wretched willow.

A robin is singing loudly and monotonously in the woods.

Foma's gaze follows the hop's capricious movements, as it crawls upwards, twines around itself and then multiplies, throwing out in all directions twisty whiskers and light, rustling bunches of tiny pale green cones with fine, dry scales.

Foma stands for a long time at the edge of the wood, gazing at the hop-entwined willow, until at last the forest sounds, droning bees and birdsong, fill his ears and remind him again of his own sorry loneliness.

He sighs, shifts his weight from one foot to the other, as if he no longer knows where to go, glances around, and suddenly hears Andrei's ringing voice in the distance.

'Foma.'

He does not answer.

'Martyr-misery! Come here-ere!'

'Not going,' growls Foma.

'What?' yells Andrei from the distance.

'Nothing,' Foma mutters under his breath, and drags off towards Andrei.

'Quick! Come and see what I've found . . .'

From behind the bushes Kirill observes Andrei and his apprentice with the all-forgiving smile of a man grown wise from his great experience of life, which allows him to treat those around him with patient indulgence.

. . . The wagtail flits lightly over the sand, gliding on her wings, colliding with airborne thistledown, then runs along by the puddle, close to the water's edge; the water-boatman has no time to escape, and she seizes it and vanishes adroitly into the clumps of pink willow-herb.

The moment Andrei and Foma are hidden by a turn in the road, which lies steaming in the sun, Kirill comes out from behind the bushes, and, still smiling his crooked smile, walks over to the puddle.

He bends over it and sees his own dark reflection in its surface; then he sets off slowly down the road, pausing for a minute by the willow with the hop twined around it, and looks at the supple stalks as he picks the leaves off the hazel twig he holds in his hands; then he walks on.

When he comes up to the bend, he looks out carefully from behind a tree, and only emerges from his hiding-place when he is sure that the road ahead is empty.

Then he comes dashing back, notices an overgrown path and turns down it, walking with long steps and staring ahead.

He stops and listens. Nobody.

Kirill runs back, pushing aside the supple hazel branches, and wiping a sticky cobweb from his face; his cassock, wet with dew, slaps against his knees; he turns off the path into a thicket, runs at random, and suddenly halts, just stopping himself from jumping out on to a clearing that opens unexpectedly in front of him.

Andrei and Foma are standing in the middle of the clearing. Around them are blue-grey tunnels of forest shadow, cool and mysterious; thin, pale aspens, their leaves quivering, let trembling patches of sunlight fall on to the carpet of fern.

Andrei and Foma are talking together; Andrei squats on his heels showing something to Foma, who sits next to him and looks at the ground.

To Kirill's astonishment, the two of them suddenly lie down in the ferns and go crawling away.

Opening up in front of Andrei and his pupil is a beautiful, fabulous world. Dense clumps of fern surround them on all sides like a gigantic forest. Smooth, gleaming trunks; hazy half-darkness; the sunlight, broken into a myriad pieces by the glistening drops, slowly descends and streams over the flat, rooflike tops of the ferns which hide the sky.

They crawl along side by side and gaze about them, enchanted.

'Isn't it wonderful!' says Andrei.

'Not specially,' comes the unexpected answer.

'Look properly!'

'If only they could be painted blue, then . . .'

46

In the midst of the regular, identical stalks there stands a huge ant-hill. Andrei and Foma stop for a time, gazing intently at the magnificent construction.

Thousands of ants with shiny backs bustle purposefully to and fro along paths and tunnels known only to them, dragging little twigs or pine needles; whenever they meet they talk fussily like deaf-mutes, touching each other's supple whiskers, and, having said their say, hurry off in different directions.

'What about it, would you leave me for another teacher?' asks Andrei in a low voice.

'Well, why wouldn't I, if you chucked me out? . . .' mutters Foma.

'All right, all right,' smiles Andrei, then he suddenly looks serious. 'Look, what's that?' He shakes an ant off his sleeve and walks on. Foma follows.

Through the thinning ferns can be seen, soft and silvery, the cloudless sky inverted on water – they have crawled up to the bank of a pure forest lake. On the blue water quivers something white as snow, alive, dazzling, beautiful.

Andrei cautiously pushes aside some ferns.

A pair of swans. Ancient, wise birds.

She is grooming herself, her pink bill picking over and cleaning every feather and putting it in place, tugging out the weak ones and throwing them into the water. The self-assured male stares unblinking at the female, swimming around her, moving with soft, nervous strokes, his head high and steady; he is filled with the sense of his own dignity.

A slender, fragile willow branch with a few narrow leaves bows down and touches the water, as if it were drinking; it makes rings spread out over the quiet water, and transparent drops fall from it with a plop.

Kirill, stretching his neck and still smiling, comes through the ferns, lifting his feet high as he walks, and comes out into the middle of the clearing, to the spot where Andrei and Foma have just been standing; he stares intently at the ground beside his feet.

He fails to find what he is looking for.

Then, furtively looking round, he bends right down over the ground and stares into a thicket of ferns . . .

And again he finds nothing.

At a loss, Kirill takes a few steps in the direction in which Andrei and his pupil crawled away; he hesitates, and then kneels, carefully pushing the ferns aside and lying down on the ground, crawls for some way, peering to either side.

Then he jumps up, out of temper, his cassock soaked with dew, brushes off the blades of grass that cling to his knees, and walks away, disappointed, angry with himself, consoled only by the fact that nobody was watching.

As he walks he shakes red ants from his hands and neck, and angrily twitches his narrow shoulders.

The swans glide over the lake, and over the deepest part, where the water is no longer clear, but mysteriously thickens and darkens, and they become dazzlingly white.

They stay quite still, tenderly touching each other, arching their necks and gazing intently down into the oily blackness of the pool; and it is impossible to tell what they are remembering at this moment, or what they are feeling . . .

Perhaps they have forgotten about all the dangers of the world, and are held by their tremulous sense of each other, in total surrender to that persistent, beautiful, inexhaustible force which has been passed on from generation to generation and from breed to breed, which preserves, intact and pure, the instinct of love and of tragic constancy?

Or perhaps they are simply dreaming, listening to themselves and to the nature contained within them, waiting for a miracle powerful enough to turn them back into people?

The willow branch bends low as if it is drinking, and black rings run out across the shining water in all directions.

In quiescent pairs the swans are dotted about the lake, which lies motionless, shining in the sun, darker in the deep places and the little inlets, but trembling with lead-coloured ripples close to the low bank where the breeze blows.

Calm and safe . . .

And in the overwhelming quiet, now nearer, now further, now close by, a commanding, muted murmur is heard form the handsome males and tender, soothing words from their beloved: 'Onk, onk, onk . . .'

*

Andrei and Foma lie with bated breath in the ferns, at the very edge of the water. A swan sails across the lake, carefully and slowly, not disturbing its stillness. Past the motionless pairs, as if not noticing their insulting placidity, proud of his own solitude, he swims calmly, looking from side to side, assured and sober. He is already less handsome than his younger fellows, his long neck has lost the dull sheen that might once have been his pride, and his feathers are no longer white but greyish.

Something is worrying him. Is it his loneliness, or the constant, monotonous nodding of the willow twig and the mysterious rings that emanate from it . . .?

'What's he doing?' whispers Foma.

'He's the leader,' breathes Andrei.

'But what is he . . .'

'Wait.'

The leader is on the alert as he glides over the water.

In the half-light made by the bushes overhanging the lake can be seen one motionless pair, a little further is another, and then another.

The leader stretches out his neck, looks to either side, turns round, softly pushes himself off, and slowly swims back again. He moves more and more slowly . . . until at last he stops. He has a regular, straight, red-brown beak, bulging at the top and flat at the end. His eyes are observant and deep.

. . . He saw the earth from high above when the flock was in flight, through breaks in the clouds he saw cloud shadows running over yellow and green fields; dense, dark woods and sparse, light ones, with black, scorched patches from great fires, and little circles, bright as the sky – the lakes for which they longed.

The leader rotates his tail and thrusts his head under the water.

For some reason Andrei feels saddened, upset, his eyebrows tremble, and he looks across to a pair swimming almost next to the bank.

They nestle together, feeling the tender warmth hidden under their wings and around their hearts. With his beak he feels delicately through the light, amazingly dense, soft feathers on her long neck, and the wind carries them gently, unprotected and lost, towards the rustling sedge. He suddenly shudders, starts to make an incomprehensible muttering sound, fussing and agitated, and then freezes once again, tense and majestic.

She does not move, but submits chastely and gracefully to the wishes of her master.

The willow branch touches the water, again the circles go spreading out from it, and all of a sudden the leader throws himself to one side, beating his wings on the water, and utters a demanding, desperate cry.

The flock dash towards him, honking as they turn into the breeze, their broad feet slapping the water; splashing noisily and creating a wind with their wings, one after the other they rise heavily into the air.

Still not understanding what is happening, Andrei and Foma leap to their feet, waving their arms and shouting in delight at the swans as they fly away.

And then the most terrible thing happens.

The leader, flying ahead of the flock, suddenly turns over in the air as if he has struck some invisible barrier, convulsively flaps one wing, and starts to fall headlong, losing feathers as he goes, somersaulting in the air, his heavy body breaking through the branches of the trees on the bank.

The end of the leader means the end of the flock. The heavy birds thrash around over the lake, their wings whistling, and hurtle from one side to the other.

Barking, choking with excitement, dogs come careering along the bank, jumping over black muddy puddles and fallen trees.

Twigs crack as horsemen gallop by, churning up the clear water of the stream. Swan feathers fly in the wind like snowflakes.

One after the other white birds fall with a cry, and lie struggling in the ferns with broken wings.

The hunt is an enthralling adventure.

Flushed with slaughter, the horsemen ride at full gallop into the lake, the sweating horses go down on their haunches in the slippery mud, and the huntsmen raise their bows slowly, with concentration, and kill off the last of the swans as they thrash about above the lake.

Rich embroidered clothes are torn and dirty.

Faces scratched by branches glisten with sweat.

Horses stumble in response to reins held by riders, who are no longer in control.

Cries, barking, whistling . . .

Over the lake with its muddied inlets, crushed reeds and broken bushes, the wind carries a puff of white down . . .

And silence falls again.

The huntsmen sprawl on a carpet on the trampled ferns. Near by, wet flanks heaving, saddled horses stamp about rattling their bridles and rustling the bushes to which they are tethered.

A young huntsman raises himself on his elbow on the carpet, wipes his perspiring face with his sleeve, takes a beaker from a servant, and drinks; water dribbles on to the ground.

'Time to move, Prince, no point in sitting on here,' says an elderly huntsman as he comes out of the forest and glances around.

One after the other the Prince's men appear at the edge of the trees, laden with dead swans which they fling on to one pile.

The wind stirs the white silk of the feathers and whistles grotesquely through the protruding dead wings. The dogs, their tongues hanging out, pant fast and noisily, and try not to look at the game.

'Good lad, Grisha, he tracked them down,' says the Prince, throwing his empty beaker on to the grass. His face, with its broad cheekbones, glows, and his eyes are only just visible among his jolly, affable wrinkles.

'Grishka!' he calls, standing up.

Grishka appears, fat, pock-marked and smiling, in a torn shirt.

'There's one stuck up there in the tree, go and get it,' says the Prince, staring upwards. Grishka at once looks serious, takes off his boots and climbs into the tree.

'Let's go, Prince, don't delay,' the elderly huntsman persists, 'you're not on your own land, are you?'

'Oh.' – The Prince waves dismissively. 'At least let's give the horses time to rest. Nobody's seen us.'

'Ay, but your brother won't forgive you if he finds out! He'll send us to the devil's mother,' says the older man fearfully.

The Prince laughs: 'All my big brother wants is to get at the girls. He's not quick on his feet, that brother of mine. He'll lose himself on his own estates . . .'

'Hope to God he does,' comes a mutter from the carpet.

At that moment the sound of approaching hooves comes through the wood, they all jump to their feet, and out on to the clearing, with a crackle of breaking twigs, dashes a man on horseback; barely

51

managing to rein in his horse, he shouts, spluttering in his haste, wide-eyed: 'There's forty men or so just come over the river! I think it's the Grand Prince and his hunt!'

'Where?' asks the Prince, and he turns pale.

'Coming up to the wood.'

'And where were you all this time? I'll flog you, you son of a bitch, damn you,' bellows the Prince, leaping into his saddle. 'Vanka! Grishka! Mitka! Pick everything up. Grishka, pick everything up!'

In a few moments the clearing is empty.

The sound of hooves dies away through the forest.

Silence. A speck of down floats over the clearing in the sunlight.

And then, slowly, dejected, gazing about them, the Grand Prince's huntsmen ride into the clearing. The Grand Prince himself rides at their head, surrounded by richly dressed men. He is the image of his younger brother, except that his beard is blacker, and his nose slightly crooked because the bridge has been broken.

The Grand Prince stops his horse, fingering his beard as he looks at the trampled ferns in the clearing, scattered with swan feathers and down, and says with gloomy satisfaction: 'So-o-o . . . Very well, then . . .'

And the Grand Prince's huntsmen ride slowly out of the clearing.

Silence descends again; this time for a long while. Then a cool wind rustles through the tops of the trees and, from high above the clearing, falls the mutilated swan, which Grishka in his hurry failed to bring down from the tree.

He is still alive; then his neck and his broken wings quiver, and with a rapid shudder he dies . . .

. . . The earth, in the breaks between the clouds, moves further and further away, the cloud thickens, allowing ever-fewer glimpses of the familiar lakes, and at last the earth vanishes altogether behind a radiant veil of fleeting clouds . . .

4 Summons to the Kremlin: Winter 1405

Another winter. Through a narrow window cluttered with paint brushes, broken pottery, shavings and egg shells can be seen a section of the monastery courtyard; across it runs a path, thickly covered in snow and barely visible. A number of figures in black habits are walking along the path, carrying yokes, from which hang heavy wet clothes; the monks are on their way to the river to rinse the washing.

The cell is in half-darkness, despite the whitewashed wooden walls, intended to make it lighter. Kirill sits in the dim light by the window, with an ikon on his knees. He wears a coarse shirt covered in paint stains, and his sleeves are rolled up.

Kirill's eyes are red and swollen, he has clearly been working all through the night.

In the opposite, darkest, corner it is like night; over a tub of water a flame whispers on the very end of a wick, sending up heavy blue smoke. A piece of charcoal drops into the tub with a hiss, and the agitated surface bursts into a mass of darting reflections.

Kirill adds the final stroke and puts down his brush.

Then he carefully lays the ikon on the table where it is lightest, and walks over to the window, forcing himself to straighten his stiff back.

For a while he stands there, relaxed, not thinking about anything, fingering a pine shaving that happens to be in his hands.

Or is he perhaps thinking so intensely that it hurts?

Kirill crosses himself and turns, apprehensively, to look at the finished ikon. He stares at it without seeing it, thinking about something quite different. His movements are mechanical, constrained.

He goes over to the window again; wide-eyed, he gazes through the frosty glass that takes away all the daylight, and goes on thinking about the same thing, unable to tear himself away from the window, because it is such a good place for thinking about all that is on his mind.

Eventually he makes himself move away and return to the table, still painfully deep in thought, picks up the ikon, carries it across to the half-darkness by the wall, and puts it down on the floor.

He stands there looking at the ikon, deep in thought, and then goes back to the window, the hazy, dirty window where he finds it so easy to think about what is most important.

His mouth is half-open, and the objects he contemplates have no shape or meaning for him.

Mechanically he returns to the ikon, kneels down, pulls several others out from behind a bench, and places them alongside his new one.

With slow movements, as if half-asleep, eyebrows raised, he starts to pull his old ikons out from all over the place, and sets them along the wall in three rows, one on top of the other, like some strange ikonostasis, senseless and perplexing. Then he changes them around, moves away, looking at them without seeing them, and goes on with his thoughts.

The grey window draws him, lures him with the prospect of standing without moving, and thinking and thinking for ever, staring through the window at the dark, indistinct outlines of the monastery buildings.

And only when, for the fourth time, he has been standing for a long while by the dark, all-important window, does Kirill notice, to his distress, as he stares out into the deserted courtyard, that everything around him is taking on clear outlines, and merciless, logical meaning.

A sudden din beyond his door: a door slams, and someone shouts happily: 'Foma! Give me the fur jacket, Foma. They're leaving now . . . What? The sheepskin? Where is the sheepskin?'

Somebody runs noisily past his cell. And then all is quiet again.

Kirill moves away from the window, throws a rapid, sober glance at the ikons leaning against the wall, puts on his cassock, picks up a basket full of wet clothes from the corner, and a yoke, and goes out into the passage, slamming the door.

The ikonostasis Kirill constructed comes tumbling down like a pile of logs.

At the entrance to the monastery an old monk with a wet shirt under his arm stands in the snow leaning on a staff.

'Well?' he asks Kirill, blinking his childlike, lashless eyes.

'What?' Kirill does not understand.

'Had a bite to eat, then?' The toothless old man laughs. 'You listen to me, Aleksei.'

'You're muddling me with someone else, Father Nikodim,' answers Kirill. 'Aleksei went off to the river a long while ago, I'm Kirill.'

'Kirill?' The old man seems to be remembering something, his sunken mouth mumbling. 'Would you ever rinse my shirt out for me?'

'Give it here . . .'

'Piotr must be at the stream, then . . . Yes . . . I've been standing here, and Piotr's gone already.'

Father Nikodim gives Kirill the shirt and looks around anxiously.

Kirill takes a few steps towards the gates and stops.

'Maybe there's something else you need rinsed? Maybe you need something washed?'

The old man stumbles uncertainly towards Kirill.

'If you like I'll go and fetch it myself, I'll find it, don't worry,' Kirill insists.

'No, there's nothing. The young ones sorted it all out . . .' mutters the old man quickly '. . . you tell him not to, tell him not to slog. Fancy him wanting to do that.' The monk's speech grows confused as he hurries after Kirill, his staff rapping on the ground.

Kirill turns and goes out of the gate.

Left alone, the old man stops, and looks bewildered.

The ice-holes are down below, at the bottom of the hill. Several figures are grouped around each of them.

Kirill walks downhill with the basket and the yoke.

He walks out on to the ice, and, stepping carefully in order not to slip, makes his way across a narrow blue strip which glistens dully in the midst of the lustreless snow, and goes up to one of the holes, where he lays out a bast mat on the ice.

'Here's Kirill,' says Daniil.

'How I hate doing laundry,' remarks Andrei, straightening up beside the ice-hole.

'Who doesn't, I'd like to know,' enquires a monk with curly hair, rinsing linen in a nearby hole.

A tall monk remarks: 'You know, they say that at Savva Storozhevsky it's considered a very worthy task.'

A fat monk with a kindly, womanish face joins in: 'We all know they have a strict rule there . . . and they observe it to the letter, before the Lord.'

One man, so tall that he towers above the others, puts in huskily: 'Oh, yes, the Father Superior collects quit-rent peasant women and they – the women –' the man makes an eloquent gesture with his hands, 'they do the laundry all right!'

A burst of laughter. Andrei and Daniil laugh with the rest. Only Kirill concentrates in silence on rinsing a heavy shirt in the icy water.

'I could take to that kind of laundry!' The curly-headed monk laughs loudly.

'In Galich, I've been told,' someone at the next ice-hole joins in, 'the monastery is only separated by a wall from the convent.'

'Well?' The tall one is on tenterhooks.

'Well – and one monk made a hole through the wall.'

'What with?'

Another burst of laughter. The curly-headed monk is actually moaning with laughter and rolling about on the ice beside the hole.

Kirill cannot contain himself. He puts his hands, red from the cold water, on to his knees, and, staring at the desolate far bank, exclaims in a voice full of distress that sounds out of control, not like his voice at all: 'God! How can you listen to all that?'

They all stop, and in the silence only Serafim – the monk with the womanish face – says several times: 'That's it, that's it . . . never mind, never mind . . . it's all right . . .'

'How's the ikon, then? Have you finished?' Daniil asks Kirill guardedly.

'Seem to have . . .'

'Seem to have, or have?' Andrei wants to know.

'Seem to have finished.' Kirill does not raise his eyes.

'Will you let us see?' asks Daniil.

'Why, are you interested?' Kirill's face twists with anger.

Andrei lays a pair of wrung-out hose on the snow, and, tucking his hands under his arm-pits, says thoughtfully, wondering: 'Mine hasn't worked at all, somehow, has it?'

'I don't see why you're killing yourself,' Daniil says, surprised.

Foma is idly soaking a shirt in the next ice-hole. Opposite him a young, red-haired postulant kneels, gazing at the black, steaming water, his arms folded. He is Piotr.

'Your knees are going to freeze, wake up,' Foma addresses him, 'go on, rinse it.'

The postulant raises his eyes: 'What for?' he asks with a melancholy smile.

'Mind you don't catch cold. You're going to catch cold again,' Foma goes on clumsily, gazing at the far bank. Down the path leading to the river comes a young girl carrying empty buckets. Foma grabs a piece of ice from the hole and keeps it on his frozen palm.

'What colour is this ice?' he asks.

'Transparent.'

'You're transparent.'

'Well then, greenish,' Piotr corrects himself sadly.

'Greenish yourself . . .'

Andrei throws the shirt into a basket and, still on his knees, stares at it intently, deep in thought, earnest, worried.

'I see now!' he declares suddenly. 'I see it all! I'm not going to go near her for the next month, not even on pain of death!'

'Near who?' Daniil looks blank.

'The ikon. I can't see anything. Not colour, not anything else. I've looked at it too much. I've got to let some air in . . . Eh? Daniil?'

'What is it you want?' Daniil is interested.

'What is it I want? Do you know what I want?' Andrei replies after a pause, 'I want to have made one or two really good ikons. Beautiful ones. And I want to be able to look at them whenever I feel like it, and I don't want anyone else to be there.'

Daniil stares at Andrei, all attention, and blows on his frozen hands to warm them.

'And then,' Andrei goes on, 'I want there to be masses and masses of people. They are all on their way somewhere, hurrying, laughing, hawkers are shouting, calling them to buy, and you can walk along and nobody knows who you are. Then there's a peal of church bells! And everyone starts to run faster. And then at night, you wrap yourself up cosily, and you sleep. And you don't think about anything . . . And in the morning you get up . . . You know after that, your eyes are blue, like a child's.' Andrei laughs.

'Let's go to Moscow and have a look at Theophanes, eh, Daniil?' he proposes.

'We could,' replies Daniil and turns to Kirill. 'Coming?'

'No,' answers Kirill; he sounds upset.

'Why not?'

'My shoes are worn out.' Kirill displays a tattered bast sandal.

'We'll find you something to put on your feet, don't be silly,' Andrei says reassuringly.

'So you'll come?' Daniil persists.

'No,' repeats Kirill, distraught, looking at no one.

'Why not?' Andrei is watching him closely.

'Because I've got to work!' Kirill looks up at Andrei, his eyes shining with fury. 'Do you understand? Work!'

'We all have to do that.' Daniil tries to make light of it.

'No,' bursts out Kirill, flinging a wet shirt into the basket and nodding at Andrei. 'He can go off and take the air, go walking in the forest, crawl around in the grass, and sleep easy. He can do all that! But I don't need any of it, do you understand? I've got to work!'

Kirill hurries, stumbles, his voice shakes. He is terribly agitated, shivering as if he had a fever.

'However much you work, you won't do any good,' the tall monk with the husky voice says, perhaps to himself, perhaps to Kirill.

'What colour is this ice?' Foma suddenly thrusts his palm up to Kirill's face.

'What?' Kirill asks in turn, alarmed, looking at Foma and not understanding. 'I don't know.'

. . . Having filled her buckets the young girl walks slowly up the well-trodden path. Foma gazes after her and stretches out his hand, holding the bit of ice, to Andrei.

'What colour is it?'

'Blue . . . leave off,' Andrei flings at him crossly without even looking, and addresses Kirill, pronouncing each word distinctly: 'Go to your cell and pray, I'll come shortly.'

Kirill looks at Andrei with a strange smile.

. . . The girl, swaying as she walks with her full buckets, vanishes behind some snowdrifts.

*

58

Foma puts the remnant of melting ice into his mouth.

'That's it, I'm finished! Rigid! Look!' The tall monk stands up with difficulty from his kneeling position and, grimacing, shows them his convulsively twisted hands. Then he thrusts his shirt, unrinsed, under his arms, and grinning painfully walks along beside the ice-holes, swinging his contorted hands.

'I'm sick of those breeches. I'd rather spend forty days sitting in dirty ones in a cave!' he yells. '"For it is written . . . Take no thought for your body, what ye shall put on. Is not the life more than meat, and the body than raiment?

'"And why take ye thought for raiment? Consider the lilies of the field, how they grow: they toil not neither do they spin."'

But at this moment, just as the tall monk is walking past him waving his undergarments and reciting, Kirill grabs the shirt by its wet sleeve and pulls it towards him, muttering hurriedly, breathlessly: 'Here, give it me, I'll rinse it, give it me! Give it me, I tell you!' He tugs at the wet shirt sleeve and looks at the tall monk with something close to hatred.

The latter, scared, clutches the shirt, too surprised to make any movement.

Astonished, the monks stop working and watch Kirill.

'Give it here, will you!' Kirill shouts, menacing and desperate, tearing the shirt from the lanky man's arms; he dashes to an ice-hole and proceeds to rinse the shirt, splashing and letting his cassock sleeves fall into the icy water.

'What are you doing, Brother?' whispers Andrei, puzzled.

'They have to be taught, d'you hear, taught, otherwise everything will be lost . . .' mutters Kirill frantically, also in a whisper.

Along the beaten, deserted road that stretches across the river ice, a horseman is galloping, raising a cloud of snow-dust. The muffled hoof-beats come nearer and nearer, until the sweating horse, all four legs knuckling, skids on the adamantine surface, its hooves sending out a fan-shaped spray of snowy lumps. The horseman throws a cheerful, superior look at the monks, frozen beside their ice-holes, wipes his hand over his face and over the hoarfrost clinging to his moustache and beard.

'I need to see Andrei Rublëv, I have a message for him!' the horseman announces instead of greeting them, and strikes his boot with his whip.

Andrei rises to his feet and declares in a ringing voice: 'I am Rublëv.'

The horseman looks at Andrei doubtfully, runs his eyes over the monks, who stand looking on with interest, then jumps lightly on to the ice, takes a few steps towards Andrei, and reluctantly bows from the waist.

'The Grand Prince orders you to report to Moscow.'

His voice is husky because of the cold wind.

'What . . .' Andrei grows pale.

'He says you are to paint the Cathedral of the Annunciation along with Theophanes the Greek and Prokhor from Gorodets.' The messenger looks at Andrei, his head a little to one side, examining him surreptitiously.

Andrei swallows a lump in his throat before answering. 'Tell the Grand Prince I thank him, tell him that . . . that . . . well . . . I shall come . . .'

The messenger bows, with a smile that could either be amiable or mocking, goes over to his horse, puts his foot into the stirrups, and leaps into the saddle.

'Maybe you'll take a meal with us after your journey?' the tall one calls out so unexpectedly and shrilly that they all jump, and for a moment stare at him in consternation.

'Thank you, Brothers, but I want to return home. Take any helpers with you that you want,' he tells Andrei, 'but don't bring paints or brushes, it's all there.'

The rider turns his horse, puts it into a canter and, looking round as he goes, calls: 'Goodbye, people of God.'

The clip-clop of hooves grows fainter and fainter over the snowy ice.

The monks stand in silence by their ice-holes, stock-still, looking from Andrei to the retreating horseman and back again.

Andrei, tense, not thinking, but with a sense of enormous happiness, stands with his back to his companions and gazes after the dancing speck as it moves away over the snow, no longer thinking of the messenger, he has already had time to forget him.

When at last he turns, his eyes meet Daniil's enquiring gaze. Daniil is looking closely, severely at Andrei, afraid of reading in his face some sign of hidden self-satisfaction or triumph.

Andrei smiles at Daniil, uncertainly, shyly, as if apologizing. Reassured, Daniil lowers his eyes.

All of a sudden the lanky monk goes running off, holding up his cassock, leaping up the hill in great strides.

'Where are you going? Where are you off to?' the others shout after him.

'To tell Father Abbot!' The words come down from high up on the bank.

Their stupefaction over, the monks talk together in low, businesslike tones, glancing now and then at Andrei and waiting for him to say something.

Only four or five still stand there, not moving: the ikon painters.

Foma stands frowning and looking with respect at his teacher. Aleksei, the curly-haired monk, has his hand over his mouth and is looking on with merry, gypsy eyes. The red-haired postulant stretches his neck, his white eyebrows raised in surprise. Daniil looks down, trying to control the tremor in his hands.

Kirill stares down at the lanky man's shirt and goes on rinsing it.

'Well, er . . .' utters Andrei and clears his throat. Then he gathers his thoughts and goes on softly: 'So, the people going will be . . . Foma, Piotr . . .'

Kirill, kneeling in front of the ice-hole, hurriedly, with hands that seem to be made of wood, hangs the rinsed clothes on the yoke, after a struggle lifts it on to his shoulders, and hurries off up the path towards the monastery.

'Where are you going?' Daniil calls after him. 'Kirill!'

'The old man is freezing to death up there, I'll be back in a moment!' answers Kirill with a smile, and hurries on.

'Wait, Kirill!' calls Andrei. 'What are you doing?'

'I've still got work to do! What do you think?' Kirill gives a strange laugh as he makes his way up the slippery path. 'And anyhow I'm frozen, don't forget!'

'Kirill!'

'All right, all right, go on. I'm telling you . . .'

Panting and stumbling over icy humps, Kirill is hidden by the snow-drifts.

Irritated, Andrei puts both hands up to his face, numbed by the frost, and rubs it. He goes on: 'Look, Foma and Piotr. Daniil and I are going to be ready by matins tomorrow.'

One after the other the monks pick up their rinsed clothes and start off up the hill.

Andrei approaches Daniil.

'The things won't dry by tomorrow,' he says anxiously. Daniil does not reply.

'Listen, why don't we go today? Collect our stuff quickly and leave? Eh?' suggests Andrei. 'Just in case the Grand Prince changes his mind.'

'He's not going to change his mind.' Daniil grins.

'The clothes won't dry by tomorrow,' Andrei says regretfully.

'Send Foma over to collect it.'

'So we'll leave after matins.'

'But I'm not going.' Daniil smiles, not looking at Andrei. 'What do you mean?'

'Yes, I know . . .' Andrei interrupts hastily, 'only I thought – maybe you would?'

'I have an idea for an ikon,' Daniil says, all of a sudden deeply sad. 'Such an ikon . . .! I shall start on it tomorrow.'

'O-o-h . . . Serves me right for agreeing without you. I shall break my neck over there. Serves me right.' Andrei sounds lost.

Daniil smiles . . .

'Serves you right . . . Come on, or we'll be late for Liturgy, and you won't have time to pack.'

They shake out the wet clothes, already frozen stiff, carefully hang them over the yoke, and fold the bast matting into the basket. Daniil does everything slowly and deliberately.

Andrei is miserably ashamed. He feels he cannot be silent, he has to say something, or do something, to dispel the painful tension, but he cannot utter a word.

They make their way slowly up the path. The heavy, springy yokes sway rhythmically as they walk. Daniil is in front. Andrei looks at the bony back, the worn, faded cassock, the hands, grey from the frost, quietly stretched out along the yoke, and feels in his heart a yearning, frantic tenderness.

They walk for a long time without stopping, saying nothing.

The monastery bells begin to peal, flat and plaintive. A cloud of jackdaws flies up over the cloister.

Andrei and Daniil approach the gates in the wooden monastery wall; the black beams are powdered with snow.

A peasant walks past, banging the wall with a heavy stick, within a few yards of the monks.

Daniil addresses him. 'What are you doing?'

The peasant stops and stares at him, and his eyes are uncomprehending, crazy. To judge from his expression, he is the happiest man in the world.

'What?' he asks in his turn, then forgets for ever about the two monks and wends his jubilant, elated way along the wall, whacking it as hard as he can with his club.

The monks gaze after him for some time.

The peasant retreats into the distance, the blows on the beams grow fainter and fainter. Suddenly a figure comes running up the hill and across his path, rushing to meet him. They talk for a while together, then the second utters a joyful yell and waves his arms in the air in a gesture of delight.

Kirill spends a long time crawling about his cell patiently hunting for his axe, and eventually finds it in a corner under a pile of shavings and wood chips. He lifts one of the fallen ikons from the floor, sets it on the window-sill, and proceeds to chop it into little boards; these break away with a loud report because the wood is dry, and as they hit the floor they bounce, just like kindling for a stove-bench. Kirill picks up a second ikon and calmly chops it up on to the floor like the first, then a third, and after that a fourth, which is harder to chop up because it has been reinforced with wooden struts, and then all the other ikons; they lie on the ground in a heap of dry pine fragments which Kirill contemplates with dreary indifference, he does not even turn round when, after packing the axe in his bag, he reaches the threshold and goes out of the cell, carefully closing the door behind him.

In the courtyard, by the porch, Kirill bumps into Aleksei who is just taking the yoke laden with clothes off his shoulders.

'You going far?' He looks searchingly at Kirill.

'I am.'

'To Moscow?'

'Maybe to Moscow.'

The other monks come slowly up to the porch carrying their yokes from the river. Last of all appear Andrei and Daniil. A clanging peal of bells reverberates over the monastery.

'Where are you going? What about Liturgy?' says someone in surprise.

'You can stand through it without me. And I shall somehow get by without you.'

The monks surround Kirill.

'Come on, Kirill, what's up with you today, for God's sake?'

'Has something happened? Kirill?'

'I've had enough of all this . . . I've had enough of lying,' answers Kirill.

There is a buzz of worried, puzzled voices as the monks talk together.

'Be quiet!' demands Kirill with sudden authority, and his calm, unwavering gaze scans the assembled monks. 'I'll tell you the truth!'

They all stop talking.

'I'm going into the world. Shall I tell you why? There was a time when both rich and poor were received into the monastic life without donations. That's how I entered the Trinity – as a beggar lad, and that's where I met him.' Kirill nods at Andrei. 'And we served the Lord by faith and works! We did everything with our own hands as Blessed Sergei Radonezhsky taught. And we gained our daily bread with the sweat of our brow. Sergei died, and it all started to degenerate.

'Why did we leave the Trinity? Andrei? Daniil? Eh? You're not saying. It was because the Brothers began to put their own interests before their faith. They forgot why they ever entered the cloister! Nikon, the Abbot, started to trade. The monastery became like a bazaar. And so we left . . . Well, and what about here? Who ploughs the monastery fields? Our brothers from among the laiety, peasants, because all of them are up to the ears in debt to the monastery. And who nowadays allows a man to become a monk for nothing? What about you, slave of God, what did you pay for the monastic life?' He turns to a plump-faced monk. 'Twenty serfs, or thirty? And you? Did you come many times to bargain with the Abbot? For two water meadows – or perhaps it was only one – you bought yourself eternal bliss, did you? You all know this without my telling you, only you don't say anything, you pretend not to notice, because life in the community is so peaceful, it's no trouble.'

Kirill pauses for breath, and wipes his face with his hand.

'And maybe I would not say anything either, maybe I would put up with this abomination if only . . . if only I had talent. In fact not even talent – if I had even the slightest ability for painting ikons. But the Lord did not give me talent, thanks be to God!' Kirill smiles, he is terribly agitated. 'And I am happy to be without talent, only for that reason am I honest, and pure in the sight of God.'

The crowd of monks stirs, simmering and threatening.

Then Kirill raises his eyes heavenwards and declares; 'Lord! If there is the slightest untruth in what I have just said, send punishment down on me!'

The last note of the bells dies away in a whimper, and a ringing silence descends. Only a dog can be heard barking somewhere beyond the monastery wall.

'There,' says Kirill, and, walking through the group of monks who stand aside, letting him pass, he goes over to the gates. 'Farewell, people of God, we shan't meet again!'

The monks watch in silence as he approaches the gates and opens the wicket. He stands for a moment, holding the handle, and then turns towards the porch and shouts:

'It is said: "And Jesus went into the temple and began to cast out them that sold and bought in the temple, and overthrew the tables of the money-changers, and the seats of them that sold doves; and he said unto them, is it not written, My house shall be called a house of prayer? But ye have made it a den of thieves."'

The wicket-gate slams. The monks stand in silence by the porch, not moving.

The road meanders drearily over the boundless, empty, snowy plain. Along it walks Kirill with a firm, unhurried step. Behind him a mangy dog is ambling along in his tracks. There is a string round its neck, and the end is dragging over the snow.

Kirill stops to tie up his torn bast shoe, and glances round; he picks up a lump of frozen horsedung from the ground and flings it at the cur. It cowers on the ground, its tail between its legs, but does not go away. Kirill walks on, towards the spot where the road disappears on the borderline between the low, dark sky and the high, white earth,

*

. . . Darkness is falling. Gradually the road beneath his feet begins to merge with the bluish snow of the fields, and more and more often Kirill goes off it into the rough ground at the side. The dog follows persistently behind him.

A few yards from the road four or five slender trees emerge spectrally from the blue twilight.

Kirill stops, without looking round. He can sense that the cur is coming closer and closer. He turns stealthily and sees the dog two paces away from him. He makes a sudden sideways leap and manages to land with his foot on the end of the string.

Kirill moves quickly, efficiently. He pulls the dog, whimpering and resisting, towards the trees. As he drags it he keeps finding himself sinking up to the waist in virgin December snow.

Then he ties the dog to a tree, and stands for a few moments as he remembers something, biting his lip. He looks round. Nobody. Then Kirill takes the axe from his bag and begins to cut down a fragile young tree that crackles in the frosty air.

The dog stares at him with uncomprehending eyes, miserably moving his lumpy eyebrows.

Intently, Kirill cuts off a long, heavy stick, carefully removes the twigs, chops off the brittle end, and makes for the dog.

Piercing, plaintive yelps are carried over the fields, growing more urgent and shrill with every blow, until suddenly they become feebler, quieter, then barely audible, and at last die out altogether.

Kirill throws the stick into the snow with revulsion and wipes his bitten lips with his sleeve.

5   The Argument: Summer, Autumn, Winter, 1405

A quiet, motionless evening over Moscow River; the water flows noiselessly, dark and steamy after the heat of the day; on one side rises a white sand bank, with rushes standing up out of the water and quivering from the pressure of the current far below the surface.

Sunlight falls on the smooth water beside the bank, and lights up the orange tips of fir trees in the nearby woods.

Three figures – Theophanes, Andrei and Foma – are walking along the path by the river, which is greyish and still warm.

Theophanes is out of temper, worked up and irritated; his untidy grey hair protrudes in tufts from under his angular cowl, his cassock is covered in paint stains. Andrei is walking behind him with his hands behind his back; he too has been infuriated by the conversation they have just had, and is trying to ignore Theophanes. Foma brings up the rear, pretending to be engrossed in the ground beneath his feet (he is staring at it and frowning), but he can hardly conceal his interest in the argument between the two ikon painters.

They walk for a long while along the riverbank, and when the silence becomes unbearable Theophanes stops abruptly and, without looking at anyone, demands angrily: 'Did you take the glue off the fire?'

Foma and Andrei exchange quick glances, and then Foma goes tearing off, running in a straight line across the meadow, back in the direction from which they have come.

Andrei is the first to break the silence.

'How else could it be?'

Theophanes does not answer; he turns and walks on.

For a time Andrei follows him in silence. Then he bursts out again.

'It's surely not possible any other way.' He sounds incredulous.

Theophanes stops abruptly.

'That's enough. Stop it. See that?' He stretches out his hands. His paint-stained fingers are trembling. 'After this kind of edifying conversation my hands shake. It takes me a week to recover.'

'All right,' Andrei agrees calmly.

Theophanes makes his way down to the river, crouches down, and washes his hands in the warm, evening water. Andrei is standing on the path, patiently untying the knot in the rope around his waist.

'What?' Theophanes suddenly turns to him.

'I didn't say anything . . .' answers Andrei, and starts pulling his cassock over his head.

Foma comes running up panting; he immediately starts undressing, with an enquiring glance at the monks.

Suddenly Theophanes brings his palm down on to the water as hard as he can and says angrily, by way of conclusion: 'How obstinate you are, Andrei, God forgive me!'

Foma jumps naked into the slow, dark river; his body, heated from running, is embraced by the water, caressed, gently pushed upwards from below.

He swims underwater with his eyes open.

Long tresses of water-weed twist lazily in the current; pulsating, silver bubbles bob up from the riverbed and travel obliquely to the surface; a glistening shoal of small, swift roach flash as they dart to one side and then halt, to stay quite still in the dying underwater sunlight.

In Foma's ears there is a ringing, and a kind of hiss, and a taut, low knocking: the water world is alive with its own mysterious noises.

The riverbed sinks deeper and deeper, vanishing in the misty density of the water, inaccessible and alluring.

Foma gives a powerful push with his legs and flings his arms sharply apart, so that he is surrounded by a seething, white cloud, and when he emerges on to the surface he sees Theophanes sitting on the bank with his legs in the water, Andrei, undressed, stepping into the river, and he hears the deafening crack of a whip, cows lowing, and the hysterical bleating of sheep: on the road that runs alongside the bank the herds are returning, raising a cloud of dust.

'And where, where have you seen such unselfishness, when everybody only ever thinks about his own arse?' Theophanes is almost yelling.

'All over the place.' Andrei dives and then answers with irritation. 'What about those Moscow women who let the Tartars take their hair as ransom . . .'

'Be quiet, be quiet! I've heard that a hundred times. What has that got to do with unselfishness? The stupid women had no choice. It was better to make bareheaded fools of themselves than to be tortured! What else were they to do?'

Andrei is standing up to the neck in water, rubbing his dirty hands with sand and saying nothing.

'There you are looking at me,' Theophanes goes on, 'and you're no doubt thinking, "What an evil fellow that man is!" Aren't you? But I'm not evil at all! I simply say what I see and know. People are blind, ordinary folk are ignorant . . .'

'But you can't go on like that . . .'

'Well, all right, only tell me honestly – are the common people ignorant or aren't they? Eh? I can't hear.'

'They are . . . Only whose fault is it?'

'Wallowing in sin, lickspittling, blaspheming – it's all they ever do! What about you, don't you have any sins?'

'Of course I do . . .'

'And so do I. Lord, forgive me, reconcile me, humble me! Well, anyhow . . . The Last Judgement will be upon us soon, and we shall all be burning like candles. And you mark my words, when it comes . . . They'll all be blaming their sins on each other, and panicking, and trying to barricade themselves from the Almighty . . .'

'I don't understand how you can paint with ideas like that in your head,' Andrei says in astonishment. 'And even accept praise. I should long ago have become a hermit, I'd be living in a cave for the rest of my days.'

'I serve God, not people. And rubbing their noses in their own sins does them no harm. And as for praise,' – Theophanes makes a sweeping, dismissive gesture with his hands – 'you know, they'll praise you one day, and the next they'll be berating you for the same thing, and the day after that they'll forget you. And they will forget all about you, and me, and everyone. It's all vanity and decay! O-o-h!' Theophanes suddenly groans, with pain and bitterness, and again his hand sweeps dismissively. 'They've forgotten about more than that. Every idiocy, every base thing that could be done, the human race has done already, of that you may be sure, and now it's merely repeating them. They're all in their "own circuits", whirling about continually! And if Jesus were to come back to earth now they'd crucify him again.'

'Come on, if you only ever remember what is evil, you'll never be happy.'

'What?'

'I mean, perhaps some things are better forgotten . . . you can't only . . . I don't know how to put it,' says Andrei, frustrated, 'I can't . . .'

'If you can't, then keep quiet. Listen to me instead. Why are you staring?'

'I am keeping quiet.' Andrei is seething inwardly.

'Why aren't you saying anything?'

'I'm listening to you.'

The sheep are bleating, raucous and peremptory, and the cattle lowing thickly as the beasts throng past in clouds of dust. Tinkling bells, the crack of whips, dogs barking. A senseless, ugly din over the river.

'When do humans gather together of their own volition?' Theophanes continues. 'Only in order to do something base. Never otherwise! That's axiomatic.'

'You mean you think Sergei Radonezhsky was preaching rubbish when he called us to brotherhood and unity?' Andrei goes on doggedly.

'Never mind Sergei Radonezhsky! Look at the New Testament. Christ gathered people together in the temple too, and taught them. And afterwards what did they gather for, remember? In order to execute him. They demanded he be crucified. "Crucify him! Crucify him!" they shouted. To that fox. And how they shouted! And what about his disciples? Judas sold him. Peter denied him before the cock crowed, and when it was a matter of life and death that they remain – they all ran away. And those were the best of them!'

'But then they repented.'

'But that was afterwards. Don't you understand, afterwards! When it was too late. And that's always how it is. First they do every foul thing they can, and afterwards they repent. It's a kind of senseless spite, at first it isn't even obvious, a demon gets into them and they rampage and burn, they're thirsty for blood, and they can't stop, they can't control themselves . . . And look at them now! It's too terrifying to think about.' Theophanes's voice breaks off in indignation. 'Lord, quench the flame of my passions . . . for I am wretched and a sinner . . . Princedom against princedom, Russians against Russians, sword in hand. Slaughtering their brothers. Desperate for power . . . deliver me from all the many deeds of the wicked . . . It makes my hair stand on end, I want to sink into the ground with shame. Orthodox killing Orthodox. Destroying churches. Leaving the dead unburied!' The old man's voice trembles, it is as if his senescent will cannot contain the youthful turbulence of his southern spirit. Andrei tries several times to join issue with him, but the old Greek no longer hears his companion, he is not arguing but accusing. Nor can he see Andrei any longer, for his vehement imagination has placed before his gaze an event which confirms that he is justified in his ideas and in his passion . . .

. . . In the stifling white dust a vast mob was walking up the sun-baked, stony road leading to the top of the hill; they were shouting, their mouths gaping and crooked, and throwing stones at a man who walked, his head held high, surrounded by soldiers who were keeping him away from a crowd excited to fever-pitch by the prospect of an execution; amongst them were horsemen, and a huge flock of bleating sheep, terrified by this mass of frenzied people; and in the midst of the monstrous whirlpool of human hatred and betrayal was the Nazareen, stumbling and falling to his knees, his face bloody; and the heavy oak cross, which was passed along on upstretched hands by people blinded by their thirst for blood, dripping with sweat, their faces grimy with the dust of the road; the cross glided over the crowd to a pit; there they laid him down on the wooden beam, fell on him, stretched out his exhausted arms along the branches of the cross, and drove black, forged nails into his palms with blows from the back of an axe.

. . . Theophanes runs his trembling fingers across his eyes, as if pulling away some film that obscures his vision, seeing Andrei in front of him once more demands: 'Where are they, then, these righteous men of yours. Eh? Your selfless people? Be good enough to show them to me. How true it is that "God is greatly to be feared in the assembly of the saints", for those people of yours, who have forgotten the faith. To be feared! If there were no fear there would be no faith! Leave me be, I can't talk about it any more . . .'

Autumn. A fine drizzle is falling. Deep in his own thoughts, Andrei is standing under a birch tree which is shedding its leaves, and staring hard at Theophanes who crossly wraps his cassock around him.

'Very well, I shan't go on . . .' Morosely, he is pursuing the argument begun in the summer by Moscow River. 'Of course people do both good and evil . . . That's the bitter fact . . . Only you can't blame them all, indiscriminately. That's hard . . . and sinful, it seems to me.' Andrei lowers his eyes. 'And it's all there, in the Gospel. Judas sold Christ, but remember who bought him? The people? No, the scribes. The high-priests. Because they were afraid of the truth, they were afraid that the people would cease to be subject to them.'

They walk slowly on beside the monastery wall in the dreary rain, their hands thrust into their sleeves.

'Look at all the money they handed out to Judas, and to the soldiers, they didn't stint, so that their orders would duly be carried out.' Andrei looks down at his feet and at the path lying in front of him, slow and smooth, beaten down with rain, and the small puddles, and grass that seems unnaturally green for autumn. His voice is calm and even. 'And who accused him, the people? Again it was the Pharisees and scribes, they couldn't find any witnesses, however hard they tried. Who would slander him when he was innocent? It was only later on that they found a traitor . . .'

'They found two, not one but two blackguards!'

'Yes, yes, two. And so? Two is not all of them. And the Pharisees were past masters at deceit, they were literate and cunning and took the people in, convinced them, incited them. In fact they learnt how to read in order to be able to do evil. In order to come to power by manipulating people's ignorance. People have to be reminded as often as possible that they are people, that they are Russians, sharing the same blood and the same land. There is evil everywhere, someone can always be found to sell you for thirty pieces of silver. But there are others who suffer without complaining, they labour till their backs are bent, doing the work of two, or three, and all the time fresh disasters befall them: either Tartars three times in one autumn, or famine, or plague, and he'll go on working, working, working, working, meekly carrying his cross, not despairing, only praying that his strength will last . . .' Andrei's voice is as monotonous as that of a mother lulling a sick child to sleep, but his habitually calm eyes are full of surging vigour, of rapture. He long ago ceased to be aware of the path, or Theophanes, or the raw breath of the rain; what he feels is the smell of snow and biting winter cold; before him unfolds the same act, the same drama, that pursues Theophanes, and every time he thinks of it, it fills Andrei with calm, with the certainty that he is right.

. . . In the frozen dawn or just before evening, a small procession of some thirty people walked slowly up a quiet winter road, clearly seen through the top branches of alder trees in which hung deserted rooks' nests; men, women in dark shawls, children, dogs running along the edge of the road after the crowd; the women's faces were full of sorrow, the children's showed they had been weeping, those of the men were severe and restrained; and they were all looking at a man who walked ahead barefoot, with a heavy birch cross on his shoulder, and at the tattered peasant helping him to bear the weight; he threw it down at the top of the hill by a pit dug in the frozen earth, scooped up some snow in his hand and swallowed it, staring so calmly at the people who had stopped below him that some peasant woman fell on to her knees in the untrodden snow, gasping silently; the others all turned round, because suddenly some horsemen had come galloping up the hill; they all dismounted except for one, who took a piece of birch-bark out of his saddle-bag and wrote something on it, while some strapping lads in boots were laying him on the cross, working away efficiently and without hurrying; several people sank down on to the snow; a messenger fellow took the written birch-bark from the horseman who waited nearby, and ran with it in his hand to the people standing in silence around the pit; a patchy mongrel sitting sideways on to what was happening raised its head and started to howl, but its wistful, dying voice could not be heard . . .

. . . Andrei notices that for the past few minutes he has been tugging at the handle of the wicket-gate in the monastery wall instead of giving it a shove with his shoulder; turning to Theophanes he goes on: 'Surely people like that are supported by the Almighty? Surely he forgives them their ignorance? You know yourself, sometimes when things are going wrong, or you're tired, worn out, and nothing can make you feel better, suddenly in a crowd you meet someone else's eyes, simple, human eyes, and it's as if you've taken communion, everything immediately becomes light and easy . . . Don't you find that? Why aren't you saying anything?' Andrei turns once again to Theophanes.

Now they are walking along a winter road between tall, bare trees, their cloth cassocks wrapped about them, their argument still going on. The argument is crucial and insoluble, it will not be settled by this conversation.

'It's not as bad as that,' Andrei continues. 'Were the Tartars not beaten at Kulikovo? Of course they were. Everybody was together, that was how they were beaten. Things like that must only be done together. But if each person plays his own tune . . . And now the Princes have quarrelled, you wait, there's going to be blood flowing, and the people in Rus are so patient, Lord! They put up with everything. They suffer and bear it . . .'

'Do you realize what you're saying?' Theophanes glances round. 'Your tongue'll get you sent to Belozersk, you'll be restoring ikons in the monastery for twenty years . . .'

'Well, am I right?' asks Andrei.

'Oh, let God be the judge of whether you're right or wrong, leave me in peace!' In the heat of the moment Theophanes pulls off his cowl and puts an end to the conversation, tugging at his shaggy locks.

'You're too young to be teaching me, far too young! And I'm too old to be taught.'

Andrei smiles, wearily; he scoops up a palmful of snow from a drift and swallows it, letting it burn his throat.

6   The Blinding: Summer 1407

In the midday heat a boy of about thirteen is lying in the grass in a meadow, gazing up through the branches at the sky. He sees the sun, and bushes; and beside his eyes – the grass; and birds, taking off from slender, trembling twigs.

Among the bushes some hobbled horses are grazing, swishing their tails. Their bits clink dully in the silence; horse-flies buzz.

The boy shuts his right eye, and everything he sees jumps over to the right.

He shuts both eyes, and it grows suddenly dark.

When he opens his left eye again, he sees a monk standing in front of him, looking down at him curiously.

He closes his left eye, opens the right one, and sees that there are two monks. They are Andrei and Daniil.

'Well, how is it?' asks Andrei.

'How is what?' The boy does not understand.

'Everything. How are things going?'

'They're going all right, thank God . . .' the lad answers guardedly, still lying on the ground.

'And who are you? Are you watching the horses or what?' Daniil asks.

'What's it to you?' the lad answers, looking at Andrei.

'Would you show us how to get to the Grand Prince's house?'

'A-ah . . . It's right here, you're there already,' says the lad, getting up off the ground.

The three come out on to the path.

'Are you a house-serf?' Daniil asks.

'No . . .'

'What are you then?' Andrei is interested.

'Nothing.'

'Then what were you doing lolling around in the grass?'

'I just was . . . I like horses,' he replies defiantly.

They walk for a while in silence.

'I'm with the craftsmen,' he announces suddenly.

'What craftsmen?' asks Andrei.

'Different ones . . .' The boy bends down and picks up a stick from the ground. 'We were building the Grand Prince's mansion. There's stonemasons, and builders, and carpenters too.'

'So you're shirking, are you?' remarks Daniil.

'No, it's all finished. We finished late yesterday evening, and today we're leaving. The Prince arrived this morning.'

They walk past the site of a fire. Several peasants, filthy from head to foot, are dismantling a half-burnt wall and piling the beams up on one side.

'It burnt down then?' Andrei asks the lad.

'They set it alight last summer.'

'Who did?'

'Must have been thieves, who else?' the boy says, without looking round, swiping his stick through the nettles growing on either side of the path.

Through the blackened, fire-gnawed ribs of the burnt-out tower the shining white stone walls of the Prince's new mansion quiver in a fluid, sultry heat-haze.

'What a beauty!' exclaims Daniil admiringly. The boy, still walking, turns and looks at the monks for the first time.

'What work did you do, Ivan?' Andrei asks him.

'I helped hew the stone. I'm not Ivan – I'm Sergei . . .'

'It's beautiful work! D'you like it?' Andrei asks.

'Me?'

'Yes, you.'

'No.'

'Why not?' Andrei is surprised.

Sergei's face breaks into a grin.

'It's all white, isn't it? It ought to have paintings all over,' he replies unexpectedly.

Around the mansion lie piles of shavings, lime, broken bricks. The craftsmen have settled themselves in the shade of the high porch at the front entrance. They are making themselves smart: combing their hair, putting on clean shirts. Sergei wanders slowly over to them.

Andrei and Daniil are greeted by two of the Prince's men sitting on the top step of the tall, narrow steps.

'What do you want, Fathers?' asks one of them.

'We'd like to see the Grand Prince,' answers Daniil.

'No one's allowed in. He's busy.'

'We're here on business. We've come to work on the ikons.'

'No . . . We don't need you. Andrei Rublëv and Daniil the Black are going to restore the ikons for us.' The soldier waves them away.

'Rublëv . . . what's so good about Rublëv?' says Daniil.

'Look, this is Daniil.' Andrei smiles. 'And I am Rublëv.'

The master craftsman is leading the Grand Prince through narrow passages with grilles on the windows, poky attics, vaulted halls. After the dazzling sunlight and the white exterior of the mansion, it seems almost dark indoors.

Behind them walks the Prince's lieutenant. They go down a narrow passage from the attics to the lower storey.

'Well, what d'you think, Stepan?' the Prince asks without looking round.

'It's not rich enough,' the lieutenant speaks in a bass voice and his boots make a racket as he walks.

'You see, Stepan doesn't like it,' the Prince says to the master.

'If it were richer it would look beautiful,' adds Stepan with conviction, 'we're not living in a monastery.'

'I wasn't thinking about saving you money. It's not hard to gild a ceiling,' the old man says quietly and obstinately, 'but as for making it beautiful – that's not so simple . . .'

'I don't know anything about it, myself,' the Prince interrupts him, 'you talk to the lieutenant here, he knows all about these things.'

'Here's the way I see it,' the master explains patiently, 'what is it that young girls want? They don't want the daytime to be dreary, and they don't want the evenings to be frightening. And so we've made the walls cheerful, welcoming. And so that they wouldn't have to light candles too much, not to have fumes, we've put the windows towards the sunrise – it's lighter that way.'

'Why don't you ask that bungling painter of yours what colour I told him to use, and what colour he put on. Eh?' Stepan is aggressive.

'You'll not find another craftsman who can paint like Gleb!' the old man flares up. 'Even in dull weather there'll be patches of light playing on those walls, it'll look fresh and light! And isn't that what young girls want?'

'Don't you go lumping a Grand Prince's daughters along with all the rest.'

They enter a great, twilit room with painted vaults.

'The great hall!' announces the master loudly.

The Prince walks quickly beside the walls, cursorily examining the murals.

'Well, Stepan?' asks the Prince.

The lieutenant walks around the hall, his metalled boots clank on the coloured paving stones. The master watches him with the air of one who is right but can do nothing about it.

'No,' declares the lieutenant categorically, 'for some good-for-nothing little apanaged boyar this would be exactly the place to live. But you are the Grand Prince! Princes visit you, and foreign ambassadors, and how will it all look to them? D'you think they don't know what's what out there? It has no grandeur, they'll say; he obviously lives from hand to mouth.'

'Watch your words, now,' the Prince restrains him.

'Of course, it may look very nice, but . . .' Stepan shakes his head, 'but not for a Grand Prince.'

The freshly limewashed walls of the mansion are dazzling white; surrounded by the craftsmen in their homespun shirts Andrei and Daniil walk along beside them.

'It was my lad came with you through the wood.' A sunburnt artisan smiles.

'And was it you who carved all this?' asks Andrei, pointing to the band of decoration stretched out along the wall, with stems and plants and human and animal figures intertwined in it.

'Ah, no . . . I did the cornices, it was my brother Mitiai did that,' says a young red-haired lad, tugging at the sleeve of another young peasant with equally light hair and a beard that is bleached white. 'He carved all the lower part, and all the jambs and lintels.'

'Look at that!' Andrei is amazed. 'Did it take you long?'

'N-n-n-n-n . . . not,' Mitiai blushes, lowers his head, and finally manages to say, 'not very.'

'Are you long out of Zvenigorod?' asks a tall man with closely set eyes.

'Nearly a month now,' replies Daniil.

'And we're just on our way there,' Mitiai's brother informs them, 'the Prince – the Grand Prince's younger brother – has invited us.'

'He was over here,' puts in the tall man, 'came to make peace with his brother. He kept walking around here, biting his moustache. And his eyes were going all over the place.'

'He obviously liked it,' says Andrei.

'And now he's invited us to Zvenigorod to build a mansion there too. Do whatever you like, he says, I don't mind how much I spend.'

'He wants to go one better than his brother, that's what it's all about.' Andrei grins. He points at a fantastic beast drawn inside a circle of elaborate ornamentation. 'This one is nice! Did you carve that as well?' Andrei turns to the stammerer.

'I d-d-d-d-d-id a-a-a-a . . .' Mitiai struggles to utter. His elder brother comes to the rescue.

'Yes, he did all of that.'

'What sort of an animal is it?' Daniil wants to know.

'A s-s-s-s-s-s-o-o-o-o-rt o-o-o-o . . .'

'A sort of animal,' explains the elder brother.

'A dragon?' asks Andrei.

'M-m-m-m-m-u-u-u . . .'

'Must be a dragon.' The brother saves the situation.

'Look at the monster he's put inside that circle,' Andrei says to Daniil.

The Grand Prince, the lieutenant and the master craftsman walk down a long corridor and through several rooms.

'It's for you to live in a house, I can sleep on straw . . .' mutters Stepan.

'What's that?' asks the Grand Prince.

'I tell you this: it's all got to be repainted, the walls and the ceilings and everything! And it's got to be brighter, stronger.'

The master stops in his tracks. Even in the half-light he can be seen to have turned pale.

'If you please, Grand Prince, may I say something . . .'

'Go on,' the Prince gives permission, but goes on walking.

'Can you paint?'

'No.' The Prince is surprised.

'Then maybe your lieutenant is a master artist of some kind?'

'Go on . . .'

The old man thumps himself on the chest. 'And I have been at it for the last forty years! Do you trust me or don't you?'

'If I didn't trust you . . .'

'Then why do you listen to your lieutenant rather than to me?'

'That's what he's driving at.' Stepan smirks.

'I have been doing this work for the last forty years! Tell me, my friend, look at this – what is it?' He turns to the lieutenant, pointing with a horny finger at the decorated wall.

Stepan is demonstratively silent, and stares at the old man with loathing.

'And what is this?' persists the master.

The lieutenant does not answer.

'Well, Stepan?' The Prince smiles; it is beginning to amuse him.

'You see!' exclaims the master, bitterly triumphant. 'I tell you, no one will make you a better mansion, and you believe Stepan and not me!'

'Yes, Stepan, you're more at home on the back of a stallion.' The Prince laughs loudly.

'It's not just a question of skill,' says the lieutenant, glancing in fury at the master, and scratching the wall with his forged scabbard as he walks past, 'the point is to use that skill to glorify the Grand Prince.'

'I am not going to change anything! Not if you kill me! They put their whole souls into this work, their hearts! The toil that went into it! They had to mess about under the ground up to the knees in water . . .'

'All right, all right,' the Prince hurriedly cuts him short.

The old man breaks off.

'Off you go, Stepan, there's something I have to discuss with him.'

The lieutenant, eyes averted, bows and walks away.

'Where's the entrance?' the Prince asks quietly.

'In the bedroom.'

The master and the Grand Prince go into the bedchamber. The old man glances around, looking into the corridor.

'There's no one here, I gave orders that not even a fly was to come in.'

The master takes a brass key from inside his shirt and goes up to a tiled stove. Inserting the key into a cunningly hidden keyhole, he turns it twice. A small narrow door opens. The old man bends, picks up from the floor a torch that has been left there deliberately, and starts striking the steel on the flint.

'Here, let me,' whispers the Prince, excited.

Andrei and Daniil are walking by the wall with the craftsmen.

'No, it was our boy carved that,' says Mitiai's brother, looking at a carved bird set in the midst of some ornate plaiting.

At that moment Andrei notices a girl peering out from behind a corner, her eyes are red from weeping, her nose swollen and inflamed. Her eyes meet Andrei's and she vanishes behind the house.

'What's the matter with her?' asks Andrei.

'Oh!' Mitiai's brother shrugs and smiles vaguely.

Andrei goes round the corner and immediately comes upon the girl, who is wiping her face with her sleeve.

'What's the matter?' Andrei asks her. 'Who was it?'

She does not answer, and walks away.

'What is it?' Andrei takes a few steps towards her. She still says nothing.

'Perhaps I can help in some way?' Andrei touches her shoulder, but the girl pulls away and shouts angrily, her tear-stained face turned towards him: 'Leave off ! Let me be! There's plenty like you ready to help!' And she runs off towards the woods.

Andrei gazes after her.

The tall craftsman comes out from behind the corner and approaches Andrei.

'Listen. You couldn't . . . you wouldn't help me, would you?' He shifts about and does not look Andrei in the eyes.

'How?'

'I was short of azure. There wasn't enough for one last little bit. There's meant to be a bird there – a blue one. And I didn't have enough and now there's a little gap, like a bald patch . . . Could you help? I could finish it off now before we all go. Mm?'

'D'you need much?'

'No, of course I don't. All I need is . . . a tiny pinch.'

'Come on then, all right, I'll let you have a bit.'

*

Huge shadows move along the walls of the tunnel.

'Look out, there are some steps,' warns the master.

'Does it come out by the river?' the Prince asks, raising his torch.

'Where you told me, on the precipice.'

The walls of the passage are lined with dark stone, decorated with an elegant design.

'That's fine work,' remarks the Prince.

'It was my two brothers, they're masters! They carve the way that birds sing. They'll take a stone without any sort of markings and go ahead and carve it. There's no other masons better than them.'

They walk on and on down the endless passage.

'Don't be angry with Stepan. I was just . . .'

'Stepan? What about him? He's one thing and we're another.'

'He's a fellow who does what he's told. Don't listen to him.'

'If you were to start listening to him it wouldn't be long before you'd lost all your skill.'

They walk slowly down the sloping passage, and the darkness parts in front of them only to close again behind their backs.

After the darkness of the tunnel the walls of the mansion gleam as if they were made of snow.

'No, you'd do better not to design anything for the moment,' says Andrei.

'B-b-b-but. B-b-b-but wh-wh-what about Zve-Zve-Zvenigorod?' Mitiai is upset.

'I wouldn't start on it either, if I were you,' agrees Daniil. 'Your eyes are tired. It's true, what I'm telling you.'

'What should we do then?' asks Mitiai's brother.

'What should you do?' Andrei smiles. 'Look what weather we're having. Go home, all of you. You've earned enough. Do some haymaking, a bit of fishing. How wonderful!'

'Your eyes will be able to rest. Otherwise you'll start to repeat yourselves, and that's the worst thing that can happen to you,' says Daniil.

At the far end of the courtyard the tall painter appears.

'What's his name?' Andrei asks Mitiai.

'G-g-g-g . . .'

'Gleb,' says his brother.

'Gleb! How did it go?' shouts Andrei.

Gleb comes up to the craftsmen.

'The devils are not allowing anyone in,' answers Gleb in disgust, 'the Prince's orders, they say.'

'Where's my paint?' Andrei smiles.

'I thought . . . D'you need it then?' Gleb looks surprised and innocent.

'Come on, come on, let's have it back.'

The Prince and the master craftsman are walking down the tunnel. Ahead of them they can just make out a dim patch of daylight.

'Where are you going now, then?' asks the Prince.

'We were approached while we were here. Another big job.'

They are nearing the opening out of the tunnel. The Prince is the first to emerge into the thick scrub of the precipitous river bank. After the darkness the bright sunlight makes their eyes water, and involuntarily they close their eyes. The invisible flame of the torch flickers in the wind.

'Well done! You certainly know your job. You are masters!'

There is a gleam of water through the bushes, at the bottom of the precipice. The Prince turns over a cobblestone with his heel and gives it a shove. It goes rustling down through the bushes, then there is a deep-sounding splash.

'Well, and where are you being asked to go?' The Prince screws up his eyes from the glare.

'To Zvenigorod, to your brother, he's decided to build himself a mansion as well.'

The Prince grunts, it is not clear what he means; darting a glance at the master, he crawls back into the tunnel.

The torch has almost burnt out, the light hardly reaches the low vault.

'We were bidden to Novgorod, but we decided on Zvenigorod. Your brother promised he wouldn't stint . . .' the old man goes on.

'So when are you leaving?'

'We've already cleaned up ready for the journey. And the stone has been taken over there already.'

The torch flickers and dies. Everything is plunged into darkness.

'Damn it,' says the Prince angrily.

'It doesn't matter, we're nearly there, I'll go ahead. I know every step . . .'

Sergei is lying at the edge of the wood under a plane tree, amusing himself with the same game as before: he shuts his right eye and sees the black foundations of the burnt tower glistening in the sun. Then he shuts his left eye and sees the mansion, white as snow, with its decorative carved columns and cornices, against the clear sky.

For a long time Sergei lies there in the grass, until at last he hears a shout: 'Serioga-a-a! Sergei-ei-ei!'

He jumps up and makes a beeline through the bushes towards the new royal residence.

Nothing remains of the tower that burnt down last year except one part of the ground floor, a few low extensions and the stable. Three peasants in tattered, homespun shirts are taking out the half-burnt timbers from the shell.

In a shed blackened by the fire Andrei and Daniil are sorting through a pile of charred ikons. On the other side of the wall in the stables, horses shift heavily from hoof to hoof, snorting.

It is dark in the shed, and the monks take the ikons out into the daylight and lay them down by the doorway on boards.

The craftsmen come walking past along the road. They are on their way to Zvenigorod. They call out cheerily, wave goodbye, and then one after the other they are hidden from view by the black, cracking timbers of the burnt wall. Last of all is Sergei, who keeps turning round.

And a little way off from the road, hiding behind the bushes, the girl with tearful eyes creeps along behind the craftsmen – apparently seeing them off . . .

Andrei and Daniil gaze after the craftsmen. For a long time their white shirts can be glimpsed through the dismal remains of the Grand Prince's gutted dwelling.

The monks sit on their heels by the pile of ikons and sort them out, examining them and putting to one side those that suffered most damage in the fire.

Andrei picks out from the heap a badly damaged ikon and looks at it, sighing with despair, and is about to put it aside when he suddenly notices a mark scratched on the back of the board.

'Look here, Daniil!' he says in excitement. 'It's my ikon!'

'What d'you mean, yours?'

'I painted it!'

Daniil bends over the ikon.

'I can't see a thing.'

'Here, look!' Andrei shows him the mark. 'Don't you remember, I decided to put a mark on my ikons with an axe, and you gave me the rough edge of your tongue. – You remember?'

'A-a-ah . . .' Daniil smiles. 'You kept threatening to run away.'

'I'll have to try . . .'

The surface of the ikon has almost completely burnt away; it is charred, the paint is cracked, it is quite impossible to make out the picture.

Andrei sets out his tools on a bench they brought out from the shed, and starts carefully removing the layer of soot and carbon from the ikon.

'How did it get here?' Andrei is puzzled. 'I don't know . . . I only remember that Abbot Nikon sent one ikon to boyarinia Khokhlova as a present . . .'

At a little distance from the monks, afraid of coming closer, a stocky peasant is loitering; a thick beard grows right up to his eyes, and he is covered in smuts from head to foot. Now he sits down on the blackened planks, now he timidly comes a little closer to them and squats on the ground. Then he stands up again and makes a circle around the ikon painters.

Andrei and Daniil, not noticing him, are bent over the ikons, cleaning them with careful, precise movements, trying not to damage the layer of paint.

'So they've gone to Zvenigorod after all . . .' says Andrei.

'I know that master of theirs, he's from Kiev,' answers Daniil.

The bearded peasant approaches them and makes up his mind to start up a conversation.

'It's overgrown, then, eh?' His hoarse voice is heard suddenly.

The monks turn round.

'What?' Andrei asks him.

'Look how it's all overgrown, I say. When the snow melted there in the spring, it all started to come up, fair pushing out of the ground. Is it the ash that helps, or what?'

The monks do not answer, once again they are absorbed in their work, irritated at being distracted.

Beneath Andrei's fine scraper the ikon reveals a tiny piece of leg and a garment. Andrei smiles, excited. 'I felt a real awe for that crimson! Overpowering!'

'It's so smooth, the colour of raspberries.' Daniil glances over Andrei's shoulder.

'Last summer, when it burnt down, nothing grew at all, not a blade of grass.' The husky voice sounds even nearer.

'Oh, yes?' Andrei says with indifference.

'And now it's all growing up, must be from the ash.' The peasant smiles. He is clearly terribly anxious to talk.

'Ye-e-es . . . I was free before, but now, see, I'm a debt-serf, so I'm humping burnt timbers.'

'Oh, yes?' Andrei does not look up.

'The devil led us on, me and some others. That was why we set fire to the Grand Prince's house.'

The monks look up at the peasant in surprise.

Spurred on by their attention he continues with a certain pride: 'I had to spend the winter in the cold pit, and they thrashed me a bit with rods. And here we're sorting out what's left from the fire, and maybe the Prince'll let us go, God save him.'

'But why did you set fire to it?' Daniil says in surprise.

'It was the taxes they put on us. The boyars were taking five from every village, and then there was the monastery. Nothing but taxes! They even started taking a tax for having no children! And the Prince's agent came along,' – the peasant is suddenly alarmed – 'and then, well, the devil got into us.'

The monks go on working, scraping away with their tools.

'Aleksei held on to that azure, he didn't give it back,' says Andrei, trying not to pay any attention to the peasant.

'Never mind, we'll get some more,' replies Daniil.

Beneath Andrei's scraper appears the hand of the Saviour in Power.

'It's ridiculous! I had no idea how to do anything.'

'Yet you remember how you kept asking? You kept wanting to start an ikon on your own, without me.'

'Now, thank God, it's stone, it can't be burnt down. You'd never destroy it.' Once again the peasant's hoarse voice intrudes.

Andrei turns sharply round to him and almost shouts: 'Look here, remove yourself, will you. Go away and stop bothering us.' Then, bowing his head, he says quietly: 'It's not my ikon.'

'Isn't it?' Daniil is incredulous.

'In fact it's not. I was mistaken.'

Andrei puts the ikon on the ground and goes to the shed to fetch something. Two of the Prince's men walk past and disappear into the stables. They can be heard calling out to the horses, and taking their saddles down from the pegs.

Daniil picks up an ikon, looks at it closely, turns it over, examines the mark, and calls out: 'Andrei!'

No answer.

'Andrei!'

But Andrei is standing stock-still by the wall and listening to the conversation between the Prince's men.

'Stop that now.'

'I can't do it, Vanka, d'you hear, I can't!'

'Shush! or you know what'll happen.'

'But how can he? They built his house for him, worked really hard . . .'

'Stop whining, will you . . . We still don't know why we've been told to go and get them, maybe it's for more work? Maybe we've just got to bring them back here?'

'Then why are fifteen men being got ready? And why have we been ordered to take lances? And why did the lieutenant . . .'

'Shut up, will you!'

Andrei dashes to the door where Daniil has just appeared, knocks him off his feet, and goes running off down the road along which, an hour ago, the craftsmen set off for Zvenigorod.

Daniil shouts something after him.

Andrei runs on and on along the hot, dusty road, panting, pouring with sweat, salt stings his eyes, his cassock clings to his knees and shoulders, flapping in the wind and grabbing him by the legs. Green and mauve patches flash and float before his eyes, obscuring the sky and the earth. A sharp pain pierces his side like a knife, and the dry road puffs under his feet, light as down.

Far behind Andrei come irregular hoof-beats, muffled by distance.

Andrei is running on his last reserve of strength. The hoof-beats come closer and closer. Past him speed some ten of the Prince's men on horseback. The earth trembles, and flying dust covers the sun in a smoky cloud.

Andrei shouts, tries to seize the stirrup of one of the horsemen as he gallops past, he is knocked to the ground and falls under the hooves of the horses in the hot dust of the road, and lies there, without moving, while the dust hanging in the still air settles, slowly settles, and Andrei's cassock turns white, as white as canvas, until the sun sets behind the forest and the road dust cools down and becomes chilly.

Then Andrei stands up.

From the birch grove a little way from the road there suddenly comes a loud knocking, inexplicable and monotonous, which carries over a long distance in the still of the evening.

Andrei walks towards this puzzling sound, turning off the road into the grove. He walks slowly through the white trunks. The knocking comes closer and closer, more and more urgent.

At last Andrei comes out on to a meadow and is frozen to the spot.

He sees the master craftsman, with empty, gory eye-holes, standing by a birch tree and knocking on it with a stick, insistent and peremptory. Guided by the knocking, from all sides, moaning, hands outstretched, his comrades struggle towards him. In place of eyes, all have black wounds; their white shirts are blooded and torn. Stumbling from tree to tree, the blinded craftsmen are converging on the spot where the master is knocking.

Numb with horror, Andrei watches the young man with the stammer, hands spread out, bumping into a birch, muttering, staggering on towards the master's summons, in the wake of the others; all are as one in their suffering, in the irredeemable disaster that has fallen on them.

They draw together in a close circle, calling out incoherently, clinging to one another, as they establish whether all are here. Then they spend some time shouting for Sergei, but there is no answer. After that the craftsmen form themselves into a long chain, the master at the head, and holding on to one another they move cautiously in file behind the master, who feels his way with a stick, leading them through the snow-white birch grove.

The one bringing up the rear suddenly stumbles, falls to the ground, and cries out, terrified of being left on his own. They all stop, and the master, his voice calm, as calm as he can make it, says something gentle and soothing. Eventually the straggler manages to find his place, puts his hand on the shoulder of the man in front, and the blind men slowly feel their way forward; after some minutes they are lost from view among the white trunks.

Andrei stands for a long time beside a birch tree, stunned, with no thoughts in his head, staring at the ground under his feet with wide-open eyes, then he turns and walks slowly back towards the road; on the edge of the wood he stops suddenly – he catches the sound of sobbing coming from a clump of nettles. He goes closer and sees Sergei, sitting on the ground in the middle of the nettles, his shirt in tatters, weeping. His shoulders are shuddering, and tears pour down his face across which runs a deep scratch.

Seeing Andrei he jumps up, stops sobbing, and scuttles off, running in a straight line through the nettles.

'It's me! Serioga!' shouts Andrei, and dashes after the boy.

Sergei dashes on without looking behind him, winding in and out between the birches.

For a long time Andrei flounders about the deserted grove trying to catch him. Sergei, sobbing, slips away from between his hands and runs away in the opposite direction.

'Sergei, what are you doing! Wait!' Andrei calls.

At last Andrei manages to grab the lad by his shirt, they both fall to the ground, Serioga attempts to break free, weeping with terror. They are both out of breath.

Andrei holds him firmly by the foot, and tries to calm him.

'What are you doing, don't you recognize me? Sergei? It's me, Andrei! Come now, come . . . It's finished . . . listen . . .'

Suddenly the boy smiles through his tears and tugs with his foot: 'Let go, let go will you, you're tickling . . .'

7 The Festival: Spring 1408

The spring woods, still transpicuous, have fallen into the dark River Kliazma. The sun is setting; the faded sky has not had time to draw up the density of evening before it lightens to meet the sunset.

On the sloping bank, quite motionless, stand transparent bushes, and the first sparse blades of grass. Beyond a rough, sandy spit, on a curve of the river where the water is smooth, still white clouds can be seen through the grey mist.

From that spot two boats appear, one after the other, from behind the precipice; on the pale mirror of river they look black. They move slowly with the current, the lazy oars splash as they are lowered into the water, creating on its surface black flashes of light.

Voices sound over the quiet water and rise, pure and distinct, above the banks.

'Hullo!' comes from the first boat.

Nobody answers.

'Hullo, Andrei!'

'What is it?'

'Daniil says we shan't be there before dark.'

Slowly, silently, the boats glide downstream.

'Andrei!'

It is Daniil's voice.

'What?'

'We shan't make it to Vladimir before dark.'

Andrei does not answer.

'Let's spend the night here.'

'Just as you like.'

The boats are moving smoothly with the current, and the men's silhouettes look as if they are cut out of dark tin-plate.

Over the hazy river comes a clear boy's voice.

'Foma!'

'Uh!'

'Foma!'

'What?'

'Foma!' giggles the boy.

'What d'you want?'

'Catch!'

'Catch what?'

'Go on, catch, don't just say "what".'

'Don't!'

Splashing sounds, a boy laughing, a cry from Foma, and Andrei's voice: 'Stop it, you two.'

And once more blessed silence comes down on the river, on the still banks with here and there a touch of green on the bushes; and again in the stillness low voices are heard, hanging over the water, like a conversation overheard close by.

'Are you tired, Andrei?'

'No, I'm not.'

'I can take over if you want.'

'No, I'm not tired.'

For a while no one speaks and all that is heard is the wooden creak of oars.

The water carries Andrei's muttered words: 'They squeak so.'

'I like it, it's a nice noise,' counters the boy's voice.

'You always have to be different, don't you.' Piotr sounds cross.

'Why?'

Silence.

'Why are you so quiet, Aleksei?' asks Piotr.

'We're not going to make it,' comes a catarrhous voice.

'Well, we shall be there tomorrow.'

'We shan't have the cathedral painted before the cold weather, we're nearly into June now,' explains Alexei.

'Let's row all night,' suggests the ringing, boyish voice.

The voices come nearer and nearer, the boats closer and closer to the shore, and already they are gliding along behind the bushes, bottoms and oars brushing noiselessly against the humped slope at the water's edge.

'Are we really not going to make it, Andrei?' Aleksei does not want to accept it.

'What?'

'Aleksei is really worried, he says we shan't have time to finish the cathedral before the cold weather,' says Piotr.

'Let's not talk about it today ... about work,' Andrei suggests quietly. And again there is silence.

'You know, if you lie like this, and shut your eyes, it feels as if someone is carrying you along in their arms,' Piotr says suddenly.

'M'm, it's true. If you close your eyes,' agrees Andrei. 'Isn't it, Aleksei?'

'I don't know ...'

'Or as if you were flying. When I was little I often used to fly in my dreams. I can remember flying along above a river ...'

'What about stopping, I'm hungry!' Foma's voice interrupts Andrei from the other boat.

'If you want!'

'Into the bank, then,' shouts Daniil.

The two boats come alongside the dark bank, rustling their way through the willow bushes. The ikon painters climb out of the boats, moor them to bushes, making a clatter with the oars; they stretch, and gaze into the gathering evening darkness, talking together, taking their belongings and supplies out of the boats.

Piotr is here, a young postulant with sad eyes; and Aleksei, a merry, curly-headed holy painter; and Sergei, the Sergei who by a miracle escaped being blinded and is now one of Andrei's apprentices; and Andrei himself. From the other boat come Daniil; Foma – taller, more grown-up; and three unfamiliar figures: two monks and a peasant couple: lay people, husband and wife.

Sergei stands on the bank, not moving, gazing into the quiet water in which here and there the first few stars are twinkling.

'Sergei! What are you doing? We're going to get wood, I'm not going alone.' Foma's voice comes down from the high bank.

'I fly every night in my sleep and it doesn't matter ...' murmurs Sergei, and he turns and heads up the slope.

Dusk has thickened. The boats have been pulled up on to the bank and things have been unloaded in preparation for spending the night. Daniil is lighting a camp-fire; he blows the feeble flame, puffing out his cheeks and screwing up his eyes in the smoke. The woman is busy with birch-bark hampers and bags.

Sergei comes down the hill dragging a long, dry log and several pine branches.

'Andrei and Foma have found an enormous lump of tree up there, it'll do us for the whole night.' He grins.

Andrei and Foma are hauling a huge dead branch down the grey, sandy slope. The branch crackles and squeaks and jumps about on the sand. Suddenly Foma stops, and stands dead-still, listening intently.

'What is it?' asks Andrei.

'Quiet!'

From the bushes, somewhere very close, comes a clear, vibrant trilling, melodious and intense. Moments later it becomes a tender, frenzied whistling, that trips over its own ecstatic trills, and in the next phrase the whistle is drawn out in one lingering breath – pure and anguished. After the first voice comes a second, timidly, as if it is being tried out.

Andrei smiles.

'Well?'

'Wait, d'you hear?'

'Nightingales.'

'Only?' Foma whispers anxiously, staring wide-eyed at Andrei.

Andrei stops smiling. Merging with the nightingale's song is a thin, barely audible ringing sound, now dying away, now coming back, so faint that it seems like a humming in the ears. The sound comes from a hillside which rises in a black silhouette against the twilit glow of the western sky.

Now it rings out louder, more vibrant, suddenly flowing into the nightingale's song, which grows steadily bolder, and the two blend in glorious, magical counterpoint.

'D'you hear that?' whispers Foma, and unconsciously takes a few steps in the direction of that inexplicably disturbing, barely existent sound. Andrei carefully puts his hands to the dead branch.

'Come on.'

'It's coming from the village.' Foma turns to Andrei, enquiring. 'What is it?'

'I said, come on,' repeats Andrei.

The two bend down again to the branch, and drag it, dry and rustling, towards the greyish smoke of the dully flickering fire.

Darkness. The travellers take their leisurely meal in silence around the humming flames. A chill smell of slime wafts from the river; close by the bank a fish splashes; the windfall branches crackle and fall apart in red sparks, which fly up with the smoke into the glowing night sky.

They all try not to look up, towards the village. There on the hillside the first, misty bonfires have been lit, and the feeble breeze carries down to the boats a discordant, alluring jumble of ringing sounds, mysterious, indefinable noises and occasional voices. They so long to turn round and look towards the village, that they almost feel an ache at the back of the neck.

Daniil is the first to break the lull in the conversation, a lull heavy with hypnotic, disturbing, delicious sounds brought by the tentative, fragrant wind.

'So what are you thinking of doing with the west wall?' He turns to Andrei.

'The west wall?' Andrei asks, puzzled.

'Yes.'

'Why the west wall? We'll paint the Last Judgement, like on the others,' replies Andrei in a detached tone.

Daniil watches Andrei slowly chewing his bread; in the oscillating glow of the fire his face seems terribly agitated and tense.

'The cathedral must be two hundred years old, not any less,' says the lay ikon painter. His pock-marked wife keeps glancing round guiltily in the direction of the village and making tiny, rapid signs of the cross.

'You know,' Daniil persists, 'I was thinking . . . what if we were to put all the righteous up there, m'm?'

'Daniil, forgive me,' says Andrei, not raising his eyes, 'I can't talk about that today, I just cannot. Forgive me.'

The strange clanging from the village harmonizes with a burst of amorous ecstasy in the nightingale's song. There seem to be three of them now, or even four.

'Oh, Lord! Those heathens!' mutters the woman angrily.

'We shouldn't have stopped here,' comes a miserable voice from the darkness.

'They're playing the devil's games . . . Lord forgive us!' The layman concludes the conversation with a yawn, stands up and walks over to one of the boats: 'Let's turn in, Maria!'

The woman nods, but she goes on sitting there, and keeps glancing towards the hill.

'They are nothing to do with us and we are nothing to do with them,' says Daniil.

Foma stands up and takes a few paces away from the fire, but is stopped by Daniil.

'Where are you off to, Foma?'

'Nowhere,' answers the latter, and returns to the fire.

'Well, time to sleep,' says Daniil, standing up. 'Foma, Sergei, Piotr! Say your prayers and get to sleep!'

One by one they move away, until Andrei is left by the camp-fire, with only the woman, still nagged by curiosity, and Aleksei, whose head is nodding with sleep right beside the fire.

'Ye-es, we shan't have the painting done before the cold sets in,' he murmurs, settling himself more comfortably. 'It's nearly the end of May, nearly the end of spring . . .'

'What a sky there was today! I haven't seen a blue like that in ages,' Andrei answers irrelevantly, and walks a few steps in the crisp, dewy grass. Now the whole hillside is aglow with smokey bonfires, and from downstream come indistinct cries, shrieks, laughter. And the bitter bird-cherry rings with the nightingales' frenzied song.

'Maria!' shouts the layman from the boat. 'Bring some water!'

The woman, her eyes fixed on Andrei, takes a jug and goes to the river.

Andrei glances round. Beyond the fire he glimpses Foma's languid figure disappearing behind a boat, following Daniil's injunction.

Andrei stands without moving for a while, then goes over to the camp-fire. Aleksei is asleep. Andrei lays a few thick branches on the fire and, without looking round, walks off towards the hill; dotted with bonfires, some large and some tiny, the hill is alive with song, incantation, laughter and moaning.

The black ploughland comes lower and lower. Andrei moves slowly up the road leading to the village, constantly pausing to listen.

The village is its own world, stirring with half-heard sounds, talk, garbled whispering, and burning its mysterious fires which throw their dancing light on to the top branches of the trees spread out over the starlit sky.

Tender shoots bursting open to throw out garlands of buds and

95

leaves, black branches entangled reasonably, naturally – supple, free, bearing their own rustling, recurring destiny; the sky, up-turned in puddles carved up by passing wheels; the mist climbing the hill together with Andrei along the road that brings him out among thatched roofs bursting with the reflected, nervous light of festive bonfires; he is weak, his heart faint with anticipation; the warm breath of fire-heated earth chafes his soul, while the voices, mysterious and clear, reinforce his own well-defined awareness and thoughts.

Plangent bells in the hands of a naked woman running round and round her house to save it from all yellow and black diseases, her laughing, naked children, doing their best to keep up with her and, unaware of the full seriousness of their mission, squealing and giggling at this supremely important moment; exhilarating flames of the bonfire beside the house, where an old woman throws a cloak over her, and, her toothless mouth smiling, leads her triumphantly back into the house which is now protected by her spell from all illness for an entire year,

and Andrei sees crackling fires, searing the smiling faces bent over the orange flames, and round them in a circle with frenetic cries, full of joy, whirl lads and lasses, their garments flying,

and a slender birch, fresh with its first leaves, leaning towards the fire, while young women and lasses, hurrying, vying to be fastest, tie on to each twig ribbons made from canvas rag,

and a naked horseman, galloping bareback to the river on a white horse with long mane and flying tail, bathed in the light of the round, silver moon, that has just risen over the far bank,

and the naked, strong young bodies of lads and girls running along knee-deep in water radiant with moonlight,

and the neigh of the horse as it dashes at full gallop to the river,

and laughter,

and shrieks,

and the sweep of arms white as chalk in the black night air,

and the slow, heavy embrace of a couple in the soft, fertile, open, good earth, surrounded by solemn, silent people in love with the ploughland,

all this leads Andrei, breathless, down to the river where he almost bumps into a young woman with flowing, loose hair, stand-ing behind a bush at the edge of the water, naked, unafraid,

1. After news reaches the Andronnikov Monastery that Andrei Rublëv has been invited to assist Theophanes the Greek, Rublëv's colleague Kirill (Ivan Lapikov) grimly studies his own paintings before leaving the monastery in a fury.

2. Pausing on the journey to Vladimir along the River Kliazma, Andrei Rublëv (Anatoly Solonitsyn) investigates with mingled fascination and disgust the pagan festivities at a nearby village.

3. The 'witch', Marfa, rescues Rublëv from villagers who tie him up for spying on their heathen rituals. She makes advances to him, and, later, with a scratched face, he runs from her.

4. Rublëv entertains the unruly daughter of the Grand Prince (Yuri Nazarov), who has come to inspect his newly completed mansion.

5. One of the craftsmen blinded on the road to Zvenigorod on the orders of the Grand Prince. (This is a shot from the original version of the scene, later re-edited to reduce the horrific impact.)

6. As one of his acolytes reads in the Scriptures that 'woman was created for man', Rublëv is joined at the entrance to the Cathedral of the Dormition at Vladimir by the deaf and dumb peasant girl (Irma Rausch Tarkovskaya). (This shot does not appear in shortened versions of the film.)

7. The Tartars break into the town of Vladimir, guided by the Grand Prince's rebellious brother, who, during the attack, is haunted by guilt for what he has done to his fellow-countrymen.

8. The Tartar Khan (Bolot Eishelanev), in a scene inserted in the final screenplay, studies with amusement what remains of the decorations in the Cathedral at Vladimir. 'How can she be a virgin if she has a son?' he asks. 'Strange things happen in Russia!'

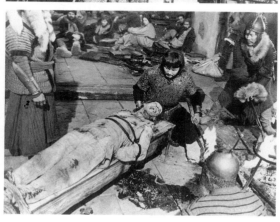

9. The cathedral sacristan, Father Patrikei (Yuri Nikulin), is tortured by the Tartars but refuses to reveal where the cathedral's treasure is hidden. Instead, he bitterly accuses the Prince of betrayal.

10. The young bell-maker Boriska (Nikolai Burlyaev) scorns the silverware sent by the Grand Prince to be melted down for the great bell. Delighted at his own audacity, he declares: 'There's not enough! Tell the Prince not to be so miserly . . .'

11. The Grand Prince, with his Captain of the Guard, Stepan (left), and an important Italian guest, coldly contemplates the exhausted Boriska, who faces execution if the new bell fails to ring.

12. Boriska reveals to Rublëv that his father never divulged the secret of bell-making. Consoling him, Rublëv suggests (in the final form of the screenplay) that they work as a team for the glory of God.

looking at Andrei with surprise, tenderness, joyful astonishment, as she stand motionless at the water's edge and puts her hands over her heavy, high breasts.

She looks at Andrei and sees that he will come towards her, hands outstretched, touching her face, embrace her tenderly, firmly, finding her lips with his hot mouth, and she will feel the coarse cloth of his cassock, her back tickled by the rough spring grass and last year's noisy leaves.

And Andrei looks at her and sees that she will come towards him, shameless, eyes wide open, with moonlight on her wet hair, come right up to him, embrace him, pressing her cold, trembling body against his, kissing him with her cool, soft lips, moaning, and drawing him down with her on to the rustling earth that smells of mouldy toadstools and the first grass.

For a long while they stand gazing at each other, guarded, biding their time.

Then Andrei turns and walks away.

She stares after him, smiling, then someone takes her by the hand and pulls her into the current, into the cold, gleaming water.

Andrei comes out on the other side of the village and throws himself down on to a haystack.

Early morning, very early. Mist is spreading over the river and creeping up to the village. The sun has not yet risen.

Andrei steals noiselessly through the sleeping village, which is sunk in the languor that follows love-making.

Grateful moans, tender whispers, the breathing of people asleep, soft, happy laughter, come floating from every barn, from beneath every dew-laden bush.

The village street is long, and he endlessly makes his way down it, like a thief.

At the edge of the village he passes an old woman sitting on a log beside a gate. The old woman takes no notice of Andrei, she is staring straight ahead with lustreless eyes at the river winding below her, at the strip of grey sky that is turning to pink, and weeps her last, cloudy tears. She weeps because this morning has turned out to be so like another equally quiet, languorous morning that happened many, many years ago.

Andrei walks down the road towards the river; beside it, looming in the mist, hobbled horses are grazing.

The ikon painters are sitting on the bank waiting for him. The boats are already in the water, loaded with chattels.

Apart from the woman who, head lowered, is rapidly crossing herself, they all look at him, intent and demanding. Andrei looks wearily from one to the other and asks in a voice that is defiant from embarrassment: 'Why are you all staring?'

'Where were you?' asks Foma, standing up.

'There's an onion there in the ashes, have it if you want,' Daniil interrupts Foma.

'Where were you then?' Foma insists.

Andrei looks at him and kneels down beside the fire. He digs out the onion with his fingers from the warm embers and, peeling it carefully and meticulously, proceeds to eat it, not hurrying, full of concentration.

They all watch him.

Foma goes over to the dead fire and sits down, his chin resting on his fists, and directs a hostile look at Andrei.

Some way from the road come riding a dozen or so horsemen – soldiers and peasants; amongst them can be seen one or two black monastic habits. Clattering over the bridge across the stream the cavalcade turns off towards the village and disappears into the mist.

'Praise be to God!' The pock-marked woman smiles spitefully.

'Now they're going to get what's coming to them . . .' adds the layman grimly.

'Let them, let them! I'd burn and drown the lot of them, the wicked heathens!' the woman gleefully cuts him short.

Andrei rises from his knees and walks towards the boats.

And once again they are sailing down the river. In the first boat Daniil is sitting next to Andrei, Aleksei is rowing, Foma is in the prow. They float through the mist past thick bushes that hang down over the water.

'Well, are you going to work today?' asks Daniil.

Andrei shakes his head.

'And will you be able to tomorrow?'

'I don't know.'

'What about the day after?'

Andrei does not answer.

At that moment from the bushes on the bank comes a chorus of yells: 'There she is! Here they are! Give her here!'

The monks in the boats look up in alarm, but can see nothing through the thickets. They can only hear the crackle of twigs, shouts, and then a cry of pain, sounds of people struggling, blows, a woman sobbing, then groans and breathless men's voices, hoarse with fury: 'Bring her along, the little darling, there, along the bank!'

The bushes on the bank come to an end, and they see the soldiers and monks dragging a squirming peasant, dressed only in hose, from the undergrowth, and a woman in a tattered short shirt which shows her white calves.

A little to one side stand two stakes hurriedly dug into the ground, and the soldiers are fetching bundles of wood and kindling in breech-bands.

The ikon painters look on from the boats, curious and horrified.

'Why are they doing that to them?' asks Sergei, stammering and pale.

'Because they don't believe in the one true God, they don't worship him, cursed heathen . . .' the woman answers, speaking very fast.

'They're going to burn them,' whispers Daniil.

On the bank the young woman's hands are being twisted behind her back, and she lets out a thin, plaintive cry, closing her eyes.

Piotr screws up his eyes and mutters a prayer.

'Why are they doing that!' shouts Sergei.

'Don't look, Sergei, d'you hear me, don't look!' shouts Andrei. 'Cover his eyes! Cover his eyes!'

The monks jump up, the boats rock violently, almost capsizing.

Suddenly the lad on the bank tears himself free, kicks one of the soldiers in the stomach, and throws himself on the peasants who are dragging the young woman over to the stake. For a moment the young woman freezes, then she throws herself forward, straining her strong body, tears herself out of the peasant's grasp, slips out from the iron embrace of an enormous monk, and plunges into the cold, mist-covered water.

'Catch her! Have you gone daft, or what?' comes a shout from the bank. Four men throw themselves on to the lad in his bloodstained hose, and he gasps and bites as he tries to break free, shouting: 'Marfa! Swim! Swim, swi-i-im! Marfa-a-a-a!'

The witch, flinging her arms high, swims through the mist over the black water.

Stones and sticks come flying after her. Now a stone lands on her head, and she vanishes for a few moments under the surface, then bobs up again and swims rapidly, overarm, her flaxen hair carried downstream by the current.

One of the men on the bank starts to tear off his clothes, but is stopped by a sober shout: 'What are you doing? She'll have you drowned in no time!'

Foma gathers the howling Sergei in his arms and puts his hand over his mouth, reassuring him and murmuring into his ear.

The witch comes close to the boat. Andrei looks at her and can hardly believe his eyes – she is the one he saw in the night, his shame, his sin, his dream . . .

She swims fast, not tiring, gazing at him with her steady, grey eyes, snorting like an animal, her nostrils quivering. Her young, frenzied body is refracted and fluid in the green water.

Andrei lowers his eyes and starts to murmur a prayer.

She swims past him, towards the opposite bank, followed by strained, despairing cries: 'Marfa-a-a-a! Marfa! Swi-i-i-im!'

Marfa swims further and further, and the mist, rising from the water, hides her from her pursuers.

The sun rises over Kliazma. Day has begun.

8   The Last Judgement: Summer 1408

Under the great vaults of the Cathedral of the Assumption it is cool, and hollow sounding. Through the narrow windows can be seen a bright summer sky and tree-tops which appear in the sunlight to be of two colours: dazzling white where they are touched by the sun and black in the shadow.

The interior of the cathedral is sheer whitewash. Along two walls scaffolding rises almost to the ceiling, dividing the white surface into regular horizontal strips.

The sun's rays fall in oblique triangles on to the floor, warming the chipped flagstones scattered with sand, shavings and lime.

Rublëv's painters are limp from the sultry heat. On the edge of a wooden box full of lime mixture, sits Foma, absorbed in a tattered design for an ikon. For some time he examines the drawing in the book intently, then he sighs, puts it aside, and gazes around the cathedral.

Daniil, deep in thought, stares at the clean wall, then he lowers his head and slowly walks along beside the wall, his arms folded behind his back.

Sergei is sitting on the third level of the scaffolding, his bare feet dangling, and leaning his cheek against a rough pine upright.

The layman, Grigori, has seated himself on the floor by a wall, his knees drawn up under his chin, his shaggy head resting on his arms, and his eyes closed. He looks as if he is asleep.

Only Piotr is working. With great concentration he is putting primer over and over on the same place, which is already perfectly primed, as indeed is the whole wall. Piotr works with remarkable determination and patience, quietly assured and hopeful of the morrow.

No one speaks. All that can be heard in the silence is the loud slap of whitewash and the scrape of the trowel.

Gloomily Foma runs his eyes all round the cathedral and calls loudly: 'Aleksei!'

Grigori, who looked as if he were sleeping, raises his quick, alert eyes. The word booms out, thrown from wall to wall, and dies away in the lethargic, airless heat. Aleksei does not answer. Foma opens the illustrated book once again, laying it on his knees. Like a delayed echo from somewhere above him comes a shout from Sergei: 'Aleksei!'

They all raise their heads, cautiously, suspiciously.

'Eh? What d'you want?' Aleksei's sleepy, tousled head hangs down from the very top level of scaffolding.

'Weren't you the last to see him this morning?' asks Foma.

'Who?'

'"Who" . . . him. You were the last to see him.'

'Well, what . . .'

'Where was he going?'

'How should I know . . . To the river, probably.'

'To the river. All right then.'

Somebody laughs.

Foma buries himself once more in the design. Aleksei's head vanishes. Piotr comes over to the box on which Foma is sitting.

'Budge over.' He wants Foma to move so that he can take some whitewash.

'You're only stirring the stuff around. What's the point?' Foma frowns as he stands up.

'There's a little bit that's not quite done . . .' says Piotr, as if to justify himself, raising his eyebrows. Having collected his mixture he goes off again into his corner, full of 'little bits' to be finished, and a moment later the liquid slapping and metallic scrapes are heard again.

'I've got a headache,' the gloomy voice of the invisible Aleksei comes from under the vaults.

'Go on, sleep a bit longer!' advises Grigori without raising his head. 'It's because you sleep too much that you've got a headache.'

'How can it be from sleeping too much when I haven't been able to sleep at night for the last two weeks, I've been going through misery.'

'What do you do at night, then?' asks Foma with interest.

'Nothing! I lie there staring.'

'What at?' asks Sergei.

'It's not so bad with your eyes open,' Aleksei shares his sad experience. 'If you shut your eyes, though, you get all these little green moth things dancing in front of your eyes . . .'

'If you didn't sleep in the daytime you'd sleep at night,' says Daniil solicitously.

'It's going to thunder, that's for sure . . .' says Grigori in a hoarse, moaning voice, leaning back against the wall.

'Father Daniil!' calls Sergei from above.

'What is it?'

'Can I run and have a swim?' asks the boy.

'No, you may not,' Daniil refuses.

'I'll be quick.'

'I said you were not to go.'

'But it's hot . . .' whines Sergei.

'Rubbish, it's not hot at all.'

'Maybe he really is hot?' Piotr turns away from his work.

'Why should only he be hot?' asks Daniil.

'Well, I am,' declares Piotr.

'Of course, he's sitting there and you're working.' Daniil starts to lose his temper.

'Let him go and swim.' Foma comes to Sergei's defence.

'No, it's no good spoiling him!' comes Aleksei's voice from up above. 'Let him sit it out with the rest of us.'

'And you can shut up!' Foma shouts at him. 'You spend the whole day sleeping like a cat, you only come down from there to grab something to eat or to answer the call of nature!'

'What have you done about it, eh, did you find any work for me?' reports Aleksei, stung.

'You could have found it for yourself if you'd wanted to!'

'Oh, that's enough!' Aleksei's head vanishes, but his angry voice drones on. 'But if we've all got to sit here, Sergei can sit here as well . . .'

'What are you all going on about!' Piotr interrupts once more. 'If you'd let him go right away he'd have been there and back by now.'

'Give him half a chance and he'll sit there in the water till he's blue!' Aleksei's voice rasps on. 'He's got it into his head that he's hot so he goes on whingeing.'

'What do you mean, he's whingeing,' Piotr says indignantly, 'it's you who does nothing but whinge.'

'I was the one who said I was hot first, not Sergei,' Grigori puts in.

'Stop it now, that's enough!' Daniil loses patience and turns to Sergei. 'If you want to bathe, go and bathe. Go on!'

Sergei is sitting on the scaffolding, hanging his head, horrified at the row provoked by his innocent request.

'Go on, then! What are you doing? Go on, will you!' Daniil is furious. 'Do you see that?' He turns to the others, but at that moment an ungainly figure in a cassock appears in the doorway.

This is the cathedral sexton, Father Patrikei. He waves his hand and makes mysterious signs to Daniil. Every movement he makes is accompanied by the jangle of keys, which hang in a huge bunch from an iron ring on his belt. Ungainly, stooping, with sunken chest and long arms which he waves grotesquely above his head, and with wild, protruding eyes and long nose, Father Patrikei looks like an old, crazed bird – mangy and miserable. His face is covered with tiny drops of sweat, and his whole demeanour suggests that he has been drinking heavily, and that something has made him very agitated.

'Listen, Daniil, Father, while I tell you what's going on! Only shshsh!' His eyes like saucers, Patrikei presses an absurdly long finger against his lips and glances anxiously around. 'I just went in to the Bishop, to his Lordship, I went in there and – ' Patrikei makes wild movements with his arms and starts to cross himself, his face a picture of mortal fear. 'The shouting, the shouting and hullaballoo that was going on, and there was his Lordship in nothing but his underclothes, running around he was, running around and red as anything. "I cannot," he says, "I cannot take any more of it! That's it, finished!" (It's you he was saying all that about.) "Two whole months it's all been ready," he says, "two months. And all that money. All that money. And the craftsmen, they haven't raised a finger, any of them! Haven't raised a finger, just sit there doing nothing!" he shouts. "Look at the money they've demanded, and they just sit there and nothing has been done." Did your really ask for a lot of money?'

'Of course not.' Daniil is worried.

' "It's all the same to me," he says, "Andrei Rublëv, Daniil the Black! It's all one. But so much money!" A real hullaballoo, it was, with his Lordship in nothing but his underwear, and all red. "I don't care how brilliant they are," he shouts, "It's all one to me! What are they up to!" he shouts, "what are they doing! It's all one

to me!'' And you should have seen his face when he said that!'
Patrikei pulls a ridiculous grimace, and goes on, as if in a fever,
'"What do I care about Rublëv and Daniil the Black! All I want is the
cathedral painted, and none of this airy-fairy nonsense!"' Patrikei
gasps, pauses for breath, and suddenly switches to a stage whisper,
rolling his eyes. 'He's sent a messenger off to the Grand Prince with
a complaint, sent a messenger to the Grand Prince himself . . .'

Daniil says nothing, he is staring at a point behind Patrikei's back
so fixedly that the latter glances over his shoulder, and sees nothing
except the sultry sky, hanging heavily over the leaves, which are
quite without movement as they wait for the coming storm.

'Well? Have you still not begun?' he asks, looking at Daniil with
his kindly, crazy eyes. Daniil shakes his head.

'You know, you . . . you should, or else . . .' Patrikei waves his
arms anxiously, and crosses himself with a wide gesture. 'Where's
Andrei?'

Daniil shrugs.

'Could you not start without him? Eh? Go on, you go ahead, start
the painting without him . . .'

'What are you talking about!' Daniil sighs reproachfully. 'Come
on, Patrikei, for God's sake.'

'What d'you mean, "Patrikei"?' whispers the sacristan loudly.
'I'd help you if there's something he doesn't know, I'd tell you, I'd
help. "Patrikei!" Look at how many there are of you. If he hasn't
made up his mind – look at you all here. He's only one, after all,
and two heads, you know . . . Where is he?'

Again Daniil shrugs.

'Gone off somewhere again.'

'Listen maybe he has . . . you know what! Maybe that's it?'
Patrikei asks, his uncontrollable fingers fidgeting near his ear.
'Maybe, as they say, he's . . .' and he is talking out loud instead of
whispering.

Daniil glances round, takes the sacristan under the arm, and
leads him out into the yard.

The craftsmen, stupefied from doing nothing for so long, remain
sitting where they are, not moving, worn out and depressed.

Only Piotr goes on priming the wall with a monotonous, circular
movement. In the silence, his trowel grates tediously against the
wall.

Foma can't bear it any longer, he throws down the book and jumps up from his box.

'Leave off, can't you!' he yells at Piotr. 'I'm seeing stars because of your wall. Why d'you have to go on scraping like that?' He turns away, crosses the side-chapel and sits down on a beam, facing the gleaming white wall opposite him.

The great fields of flowering buckwheat are vividly opaline. It is stuffy and hot. The bees make a low, organlike hum in the haze. The buckwheat is as white as the whitewashed walls of the Cathedral of the Assumption.

Andrei is wandering, with a stick in his hand, through the deep layer of warm dust, gazing in front of his feet, not thinking about anything, weary of his fruitless attempts to capture his own elusive design, which, mysterious and still unformed, is already alive in his soul and heart.

Tormented and exhausted by this futile pursuit, he walks along the road which lies over the vast field like a line drawn by somebody's hand across an expanse of whitewash.

Andrei walks slowly over the field, and his writhing shadow slips along in the dust beside him; he pauses for a second, then wanders on, bewildered and tense because of the idea that keeps slipping from his grasp, making him walk faster and faster without being aware that he is doing so, or suddenly stop and stand motionless for a long time in the sun, then go back on his tracks and hurry on along the road again in pursuit of a solution, stirring up the stifling dust, and then wander on again in the heat, through the hum of the bees, losing the thread of his secret reflections.

Andrei enters the cathedral. Piotr stops working. Silence descends, except for the chirp of the martins flying around the church which reaches them from outside.

No one speaks, they have all turned towards Andrei and for a while watch him closely. Then they realize, and turn away, losing interest in him.

Andrei stands in the middle of the cathedral, barefoot, in his dusty cassock, his face black from the sun.

'Even if you kill me,' he utters softly, and clears his throat; his voice is dry and husky, 'I shouldn't know what to paint . . .'

'What d'you mean, you don't know?' Foma speaks just as

quietly, 'We've been told to paint the Last Judgement.'

'The thing is,' Andrei turns to Foma. 'I think it would be better not to paint the Last Judgement at all.'

'What do you mean?' Daniil is staggered.

'I want . . .' Andrei begins, and suddenly falters and turns grey, his face takes on an unpleasant, aged look. 'There's nothing I want, nothing . . . That's it . . .'

'Well!' Foma says abruptly, and stands up. 'I'm leaving you!'

They all turn in astonishment and stare at Foma, who takes his bag down from the scaffolding and starts throwing his belongings into it.

'That's not the way I want to work,' he goes on, 'thank you all for being good to me, and for boxing my ears. You've taught me something! But that's enough. I am going off to work.'

Andrei stands on the chilly floor, his eyes lowered, tapping his stick on the flagstones. A sudden cool breeze blows in from outside, redolent of the first drops of rain falling on to the dust, and it stirs the bottom of his cassock.

'So, you're going to follow in Kirill's footsteps, are you?' says Daniil with pent-up rage.

'No, in the opposite direction.' Foma stares soberly at Andrei as he answers. 'They asked me to paint the church at Panfuteva. It's not much to be proud of, but at least it's there. I am going to go and paint the Last Judgement. Well, who's coming with me?' With a crooked smile he looks round at his comrades. 'All right. Stay where you are, but don't start being sorry later.'

Foma turns and walks out without looking at his teacher. No one watches him go.

Andrei looks up. Before him he sees an unbelievably white wall, so white that he feels as if he has gone blind and is surrounded on all sides by an empty, milky mist which makes his comrades' faces alien and unrecognizable, black against the background of the unbearably white walls whose absolute surface, unsullied by a single line, shimmers with grey blurs, killing all hope in him and destroying everything human and conscious, producing a spasm of unbearable tension that sends his will hurtling down the slope of blind white wall, with nothing to hold on to, sliding as if on a cloudless sky, where there is nothing to grab hold of, nothing you can rely on, any more than you can rely on the faces of your friends when that terrifying whiteness has turned them into charred beams without meaning or movement, halted in their tracks by the agony of waiting, perhaps even the expectation of death itself as a result of the frustrated urge to create.

Andrei takes a few unconscious steps and bends down over a tub of thick, stiff soot mixture; he thrusts in his hands together with a trowel, and flings the stuff on to the blinding white wall.

Black stripes and mortifying, senseless wounds explode and run across the snow-white surface. Divisions. Zigzags. Splashes. The pitch-black imprints of his stroke.

Andrei's crazy gesture is watched with horror by his assistants.

Andrei covers his head with his hands and, relieved by that ungovernable burst of tense, animal hatred, he sits down, unexpectedly, on an off-cut from a beam. His face is running with sweat, his mouth hangs open, it is almost as if he were returning from the next world.

Rain starts falling. It comes down obliquely and heavily on to the road, disturbing the light dust and gradually transforming it into a muddy flood. The rain rattles down, purling among the stones, gurgling through tiny ravines in the clay, pattering on to leaves, wrapping the trees in minuscule splashes, pouring over roofs, jumping up from the flagstones in the doorway. Everything is obscured by a grey, nacrine veil. There is a roll of thunder.

'Sergei, read from the holy book!' Daniil forces his voice to sound calm and even.

'Starting where?' asks Sergei, from the top scaffolding, his voice trembling.

'No matter . . . wherever you like.'

There is a rustle as Sergei opens the book.

In from the rain, into the cathedral, comes the innocent, the simpleton. She came wandering into Vladimir, and the monks have seen her often enough in the streets of the town, in courtyards, in the market-place. She enters the cathedral as if it were her own house, hardly paying any attention to any of them; she wears a grey hempen shirt, and is bare-headed; she has been outside in the pouring rain and is soaked. She mutters away – she has a con-genital speech defect – and looks around her without curiosity, as drops of rain run down her loose, red hair parted in the middle over her large, round forehead; her clear, shining, wide-open eyes gaze without fear and without any thought.

The rain patters down cheerfully, monotonously, and from under the vaults comes Sergei's stumbling, hesitant reading: 'Be followers of me as I am of Christ.

I commend you, my brethren, for remembering all that I have told you, and for preserving what I passed on to you as you received it . . .

I also want you to know that the head of every man is Christ, the head of a woman – her husband, and of Christ – God.'

The simpleton walks slowly around the cathedral, muttering, as if holding a conversation with herself, as if reasoning with herself, calming herself; and stops opposite the wall that has been splattered and disfigured by Andrei. For a while she stands there motionless, looking at the wall, then she turns round abruptly and Andrei sees that she is very frightened, she is weeping and her wet hair hangs down making her look helpless and afraid.

And Andrei suddenly remembers the fair hair of the witch in the mist, streaming out in the black water.

. . . 'Any man who prays or prophesies with his head covered brings shame down upon his head.

'And any woman who prays or prophesies with her head bare brings shame down upon her head, for it is as if her head were shaven . . .' comes Sergei's voice from the scaffolding.

And Andrei sees heavy gold plaits falling beneath a curved sword, he sees a bandy-legged, damp Tartar slicing off hair, an unending trail of women and girls prepared for death in captivity, Tartar horsemen on their small horses, surrounding the Maidens' Field, and men, eyes lowered, filled with grief and shame, unable to defend the defenceless women who are now saving them, and who with steady hatred and pain gazed for a while at the ground before their feet, at the dust on the road, before laying their plaits on the block.

'. . . and man was not made for woman but woman for man. Therefore a woman must have upon her head a *sign* of the power that is *over her*, for the Angels.

109

'But neither is a man without a woman, nor a woman without a man, in the Lord.

'For just as all that comes to the woman through the man, so too all that comes to the man through the woman is from God.

'Consider for yourselves, how can it be seemly for a woman to pray to God with her head uncovered?'

How could Andrei forget those 'sinful women' as they slowly, fearfully, removed the kerchiefs from their heads, one after the other, in an endless sequence, to pay for the cowardice of their menfolk and the treachery of their Prince, kneeling down in the dust, so that before losing their honour as women they moved away from the hillock of womens' plaits, feeling the despairing lightness of their hair, chopped obliquely by a blunted sword.

The rain drums steadily, and the boyish voice echoes beneath the vaulted ceiling of the cathedral: ' . . . But if a woman grows her hair will it be to her honour, has hair been given her in place of a shawl?

'And if anyone has a mind to argue, then we have no such custom, neither in the church of God . . .'

Righteous and sinners, the women walked together in file, setting themselves into the law, pitching their own honour into battle, saving their Earth and God in place of the men, gazing with tearful eyes at the ground beneath their feet and at their own demolished future.

'But proposing this I do not advocate it . . .'

'Daniil!' cries Andrei. He stands limply in the middle of the church, smoothing back his hair with a mechanical gesture, smiling gently, helplessly.

'It's a feast day, Daniil, a feast day! And there you are talking about the Last Judgement. How can they be sinners, even if they have taken off their kerchiefs!'

All look at Rublëv, excited, still not understanding, but convinced that tomorrow morning, after the rain, they will start work.

The white walls are no more.

*

Andrei comes into the cathedral together with all the craftsmen, followed by Patrikei and the simpleton. The craftsmen look terrible; worn down by months of frenetic work they are haggard, uncouth; burnt out.

Andrei covers his eyes with his palm and takes a moment to become accustomed to the dark. Then he raises his head and looks up, serious and expectant, at his joyful *Last Judgement*.

. . . One after the other, full of nobility and tenderness, their faces poignantly Russian, the righteous women glide forward.

Their quiet eyes, full of hope, and their simple serene demeanour convince the beholder that they exist in reality, convince him of the sanctity of their womanly being. The radiant eyes of sisters, mothers, betrothed and wives – support in love and in the future . . .

The innocent's happy laugh re-echoes round the empty, clean cathedral.

9 The Sacking: Autumn 1408

One of the last bright days of late autumn. For a long time the cool sun fails to clear away the hoarfrost which settled overnight on the grey, dead grass and transparent woods, but by midday the rime covering trunks and branches begins to thaw, and the forest is filled with the clear sound of heavy drops that detach themselves from bare twigs and hit the hollow tubes of fallen leaves curled up by the first frosts. 'Cup! Cup! Cup-cup! Cup!'

Under cover of tall bushes thinning with the approach of winter are two mounted scouts. Before them, through the tangle of branches, there stretches to the horizon a yellow field, long since harvested, with a solitary, bare tree standing sadly in the middle.

The riders are talking lazily together; it is clear that they have been on duty for a long while and have had time to cover every topic.

'You know what "shit" is in Tartar?' asks the senior man, dismounting.

'No . . . what?'

'"Lino".' He proceeds, without hurrying, to unstrap his quiver and undo his sword.

'How do you know?' asks the younger.

'I spent two years as a prisoner, slaving for them. It was my brother bought me out, God bless him.'

He just has time to drop his trousers and squat down when the younger, standing up in his stirrups, whispers urgently, loudly: 'They're coming! Riding this way!'

From over the horizon and on to the very edge of the field horsemen come riding one after the other. Two, five, ten, fifteen, twenty-five.

The senior man, doing up his trousers and attaching his weapons as he runs, dashes to his horse, and the two scouts go careering out of the bushes and on to the forest road, leaning forward in their saddles, and are hidden by the trees.

Advancing over the empty field comes a vast mass of cavalry. In the clear autumn air, the bright clothes and gleaming weapons of the horsemen catch the eye.

The two scouts gallop along the forest road, scattering the russet leaves. Ahead, through the trees, the dull glint of the Prince's banners, armour, lances, can now be seen and the bluish smoke of camp-fires – the Russian mounted troops are drawn up at the edge of the forest.

The scouts come flying up to the Younger Prince, who is seated by a fire.

'They're coming, Prince! They're coming!'

'Tartars!' The Prince leaps into the saddle. 'How far?'

'Far enough!'

'One field away!'

The entire force is on the move as the men dash to their horses.

'The Tartars! The Tartars!' The words fly from one end of the ranks to the other.

'Each man to his place. No shouting!' The Prince gives orders to his generals, who carry them out instantly, pouncing upon the captains and other subordinates.

Smoothly, their pace never decreasing or increasing, the Tartar cavalry move forward at a fast trot. In front, on a magnificent raven-black stallion, and bearing gold weapons, rides the Tartar Khan, surrounded by his suite. The road, as still as if it were of stone, throws itself doglike beneath the hooves of the Tartar horses.

The Russian troops are silent. The soldiers' faces are reserved and severe, prepared for the encounter.

At their head rides the Younger Prince – the Grand Prince's younger brother. He sits erect in the saddle; he is chewing a twig and cannot control the tremor in his hands.

The head of the Tartar cavalry is already on the forest road, while the rear has not yet crossed the desolate yellow field. The forest is filled with the snorting of trotting horses, the crackle of breaking twigs, the whistle of pliant branches stretched across the road by the trees. The Tartars ride in silence, twisting their heads to right and left and looking in all directions.

The Russian army is utterly still. The hoof-beats come nearer and nearer. The first Tartar riders come into view and, as they catch sight of the Russians, they rein in their horses, which go back on their haunches and toss their foamy heads. There is confusion in the Tartar ranks for a short while because those at the rear are still pressing forward, and the heated horses cannot stop straight away; the disorder and jostling continue for several minutes at the bend in the road.

Eventually all movement ceases, and a surprising silence comes down on to the forest, broken only by the occasional loud plop of a drip falling on to the dry leaves.

And they stand there face to face, armed, enemies since time immemorial, Tartars and Russians. And they do not move.

The Young Prince sits taut as a bow-string, the twig still clamped between his clenched teeth; he was too agitated to remember to throw it away.

The Khan watches him from the distance, eyes narrowed, intent, his reins shortened, dogging the Prince's every move.

Suddenly a joyful neighing bursts into the silence and dies away, urgent and impatient. From somewhere in the midst of the Russian force the call is answered by a mare, and the modulating, nervy cry is followed by another, and another. The neighing, cheerful as a greeting, hangs above the autumn forest and the armies.

The Khan makes a barely perceptible move. The Young Prince observes him, and the two jump down simultaneously on to the frozen ground of the roadway, flinging their reins to their grooms, and start walking towards each other.

They stop and exchange firm, manly handshakes.

'You were expected yesterday,' says the Young Prince.

'I came across a little town.' The Khan smiles. 'I meant to go round it, but then I couldn't resist it. I'm sorry I'm late.'

'What does it matter!' The Prince smiles awkwardly. 'Come along!'

The Khan, either because he is the senior of the two or because he is a guest, pats the Prince on the shoulder. The latter suddenly remembers his chewed twig and spits it out.

A curious force is making its way along the river bank: beneath Orthodox banners gallop wild, slant-eyed Tartars, and under plumes of horse-hair hung with little bells – Russian warriors.

In front ride the Young Prince and the Khan.

'That's the ford over there, beyond that loop!' cries the Prince, pointing ahead.

They ride up to spot where the bank slopes down to the water.

'Here and to the left it's shallow all the way. Keep up left!' says the Prince, shaking his reins, and is the first to take his horse into the water. The Khan holds back his stallion and looks at the Prince with a smile.

'You don't intend to trick me?'

'You've no call to say that. Vladimir is empty, I tell you. The Grand Prince is away in Lithuania,' the Young Prince hastens to reassure the Khan and, turning to face the bank, he shouts to all the warriors – 'Stick to the left. Left!'

The horses stretch out their necks and go cautiously into the icy water; the allies make their way across the quiet autumn river. The Khan and the Prince are still riding side by side.

'The town is over there beyond that pine wood.' The Prince nods towards the far bank, screwing up his eyes in the bright glare of the sun.

'Of course the Grand Prince has a small son, hasn't he, and you've got your eye on the throne,' goads the Khan.

'We'll have to see about that,' the Prince mutters through his teeth.

'I can see you're very anxious to get the throne, but I understand . . .'

'Don't you dare . . . Where are you going? I told you to keep left!' The Prince suddenly shouts.

One of the Tartars has forgotten about the warning and gone too far to the right, blundered into deep water and now is being sucked into a murky, ice-cold pool.

The Prince goes up quite close to the Tartar and just manages to drag him out by the scruff of his neck, and set him down behind him, on his mare's withers.

The Tartars drag the horse out of the pool with their lassoos.

'You have a great love for your brother.' The Khan sounds amazed.

'I hate him . . .'

They reach the opposite shore, and their horses scramble up the slippery clay.

The Tartar who was rescued jumps to the ground and, laying his right hand on his heart, he bows to the Prince, going right down to the ground, and walks backwards, still bowing, his serious gaze fixed on the Russian Prince's eyes.

'You say you don't love your brother,' the Khan pursues the conversation.

'That seems to be our fate . . .'

'When did you last make peace?'

'To start with I wouldn't make peace, but then the Metropolitan summoned me to Moscow, and ordered us to swear before God that we would live in peace and concord.'

'What?' The Khan did not catch what was said. They come out on to the road and start to gallop off towards the pine wood.

'The Metropolitan made me kiss the cross!'

'When?'

'This winter.'

'When?'

'This last winter.'

'And what did you do?'

The Prince does not answer. He remembers how he made his way to Moscow last year at the insistence of the Metropolitan, to make peace (yet again!) with his elder brother . . .

. . . It was a winter's evening, and the frost was so severe that the air felt dry and prickly; all day he had been galloping, together with his suite, the searing wind piercing his sable jerkin, as he cursed himself for not consenting to travel in a covered waggon in this terrible frost, over snow so powdery that the horses' hooves left no trace – having left his estate that morning he was doing his utmost to reach Moscow before sunset; he urged his horse on, it turned its face away from the wind, and as it rounded a bend it raised a cloud of snow-dust that flew back into the faces of the villains who followed him; and his bitterness grew more and more intense as he pictured his brother, making his leisurely way out of his princely mansion, surrounded by boyars and henchmen, and he rode towards the cathedral at a walk, along the twilit Moscow streets . . .

'Keep up, Prince, keep up!' shouts the Khan.

Ahead of them rise the walls of Vladimir, and the army speeds its way down the smooth road leading to the unattended, wide-open gates. The clip-clop merges in a mighty roar, the horses move forward at a gallop, and still not a soul is to be seen at the gates.

Now the most reckless among them, determined to be first through the gates, overtake the Prince to right and left.

At last someone has noticed them. A little figure is running along the city walls. Another comes out to meet him.

Someone in a long cassock frantically tries to close the gates, several others come running to help. Slowly, as if reluctantly, the two halves of the enormous gate swing towards each other.

Desperately, urgently, alarm bells start to ring.

If only they can be in time!

The Tartars utter piercing yells and brandish their curved swords. The gates are closing fast, and only the leading group of Tartars manage to ride through the narrow opening, together with the Young Prince and his lieutenant. The horsemen attack the people who are trying to close the gates.

In a kind of fever, the Prince does not know where to start, and he stands idly watching the skirmish around the gates.

The small, flaxen-haired monk who was the first to try to close the gates runs off in terror, shrieking in a piercing, incoherent voice, 'Tartars! Tartars! Tartars!' He runs down the street, his bloodied hands thrust out in front of him, tripping over his cassock.

The Prince turns his horse, sets off in pursuit of the monk, catches up with him in the space of a few seconds, sees his grey face distorted in a cry, and his huge, pale, uncomprehending eyes. For one moment the Prince's sword is stuck in the scabbard, then the blade comes down with a tight crunch on the monk's neck. Felled by the blow, he falls with a sob to the ground, grabs at the limp autumn grass at the edge of the road, and lies motionless, his face turned to the sky.

He is Piotr, the ikon painter, Rublëv's assistant.

They are pushing the gate from the outside harder and harder, the two halves fly open, and in pours a bellowing, screaming avalanche that rushes uncontrollably into the city.

Again the Prince is galloping alongside the Khan. The Khan smiles, shouts something in Tartar that cannot be made out in the general uproar. 'This is just the beginning,' thinks the Prince. 'After that I'll go to Moscow and burn out my brother's entire family, slaughter all his pups, and have him down on his knees in front of me . . .'

And in his fevered awareness the Prince is pursued by the

117

nagging memory of that winter evening when he did in fact reach Moscow before sunset, and the long, blue shadows sped away from him on the deserted, frozen streets of the capital city, lined with snow-drifts; behind him his exhausted suite with a powdering of snow-dust covering their fur coats and hats, and their beards and eyebrows white with hoarfrost, were forcing their mounts on at full tilt, not shouting any warning to the gaping pedestrians because they had no strength left to open their numb lips; and they knocked down two or three, and one was left lying on the snow and the snow beside his head turned black . . .

. . . And towards him at a leisurely walking pace came the stately procession of his elder brother, who had come riding out after a good dinner, dark-haired, ruddy faced in the frost, rich and therefore kind . . .

The warriors flood into the city. Contingent after contingent, they pour in through the gates and flow into every street and lane and alley. Hoof-beats, shouting, neighing . . .

With a dry crackling the first fires are already taking hold, and the smoke rises in columns into the still, clear air.

A group of Tartars and Russians smash the bolts of a granary, and, after looting it, harness the owner's horse to a cart loaded with goods and lead it out on to the street. Women are wailing, children crying. A Tartar sets light to some tow and flings it into the straw in a corner of the yard.

In front of a burning house opposite, two men are trying to drag a Tartar off his horse. One of them is a shaggy peasant with a scratched face, the other, in a cassock, is Foma. The peasant is armed with a heavy log, Foma holds a fork. The two of them pitch into him and drive him into a corner, but just as the Tartar's position becomes critical, two of the Prince's men appear in the gateway. One, without hesitating, thrusts his lance through the peasant with the log, who lets out a violent gasp and falls down in the gateway. Foma brandishes the fork in desperation and, trying to fend off the soldiers, he retreats slowly to the back of the court-yard, repeating in fear and dismay: 'What are you doing, brothers ! Spare me! Don't kill me! I'm one of us, we're the same, you're ours . . . Brothers! We're Russians! I am another . . .'

'I'll show you what, you Vladimir bastard!' the elder soldier hisses through his teeth, and with a swift blow of his lance he knocks the pitchfork from Foma's hands.

'Help! Help! Don't kill me! Lord!' Foma presses up against the wattle fence, and all of a sudden leaps over it and goes running off over the deserted vegetable garden.

'The swine!' the soldier moans in a tone of despair.

A mounted Tartar picks an arrow from behind his back, fits it into his bow, and slowly takes aim.

Foma runs like a hare across the black, gravelike beds, but suddenly shudders, twitches, runs on at the same pace until he reaches the edge of the garden and, to stop himself falling, puts his arms around a slender, solitary willow growing right beside the fence. From between his shoulder-blades protrudes an arrow.

The Tartar grins, wipes his muddy, sweating brow, and winks at the Russian soldiers.

With a rasp, Foma falls with all his weight against the young tree and bends it over towards the ground. It goes lower and lower . . . and at last, with a final shudder, he leaves go of the pliant, damp trunk which swishes straight and for a while goes on restlessly swaying from side to side . . .

Dead bodies are lying on the ground outside the cathedral. A wounded horse thrashes about, trying to stand up. High above in the bell-tower the chimes sound jagged and pitiful.

The Prince, surrounded by his lieutenants, is watching the Russians and Tartars working on a battering-ram in front of the cathedral doors. Anxious not to miss anything, the Prince rides his horse towards the cathedral; from inside comes the sound of disjointed, fervent, singing . . .

. . . throwing up clouds of snow, he galloped up to the cathedral before his elder brother, and sat there breathing heavily, not dismounting, until at last the procession came into view around the cathedral – the Grand Prince in all his splendour, with his boyars and richly clad bodyguard; and the great bell began to peal, to be joined by the other, smaller ones, and the startled carrion crows rose in a mass from the frozen branches, which looked almost black against the cold, crimson sunset; then to the exultant sound of the bells he dismounted, bowed from the waist to his elder brother, and the two of them walked arm in arm up the snow-covered steps of the cathedral, to be met by the Metropolitan, who made the sign of the cross over them, and blessed them, and motioned them towards the entrance, whence came exquisite, rapturous singing and the faint, warm smell of candles, and beyond the doors, far inside, glinted the soft gold of the royal gates, votive lamps and candlesticks . . .

. . . Inside the Cathedral of the Dormition it is stuffy and unbearably crowded. Everyone who managed to run in before the doors were closed is here: men wounded in the fight, with blood on their shirts, old men, women with terrified children. The smouldering lamps in front of the altar are almost burnt out, and the cold sun throws a piercing light on the walls painted with *The Last Judgement*.

They are all singing: 'He is my refuge and my fortress: my God; in him will I trust . . . Thou shalt not be afraid for the terror by night; nor for the arrow that flyeth by day.'

The final hope, the final appeal to God. Amid the singers stands Andrei, dishevelled, his cowl missing, with a deep, jagged cut running unevenly from his chin to his temple, and his right hand wrapped in a bloodstained rag. He too is singing.

And all around he sees the bitter faces of men prepared for whatever may come, children's eyes red with weeping, gazing curiously at his paintings, the features of the women glowing with centuries of patience; and an inexplicable belief in happiness comes flooding, radiant and mournful, into his soul.

The sound of heavy blows. The besieging troops are trying to break the door in with the ram. The shattering blows on the iron-bound cathedral door echo grimly under the vaults.

The singing grows louder. '. . . there shall no evil befall thee, neither shall any plague come nigh thy dwelling . . .'

With a grinding sound the doors give way, and a moment later the cathedral is filled with cries, weeping, children's screams, groans – foot-soldiers and horsemen burst into the cathedral. Everywhere is confusion, movement without direction or sense; everybody wants to run away, and there is nowhere to run; they perish, trampled by the horses, or under the feet of the crazed, defenceless crowd. Wailing, neighing, shrieks, shouts, murmured prayers and unthinking voices singing snatches of psalms.

Andrei crawls out from under a gory pile of human bodies, the wounded and the dying, makes his way along the wall, squeezes through a tiny, low door, and runs through the darkness, not knowing where he is going, stumbles over an unseen step, falls and, knocking his head against a sharp stone ledge, loses consciousness . . .

. . . The Younger Prince entered the cathedral beside his brother, and was engulfed in a burst of warm air, rapturous singing, magnificence; and after five hours' wild ride in the icy wind the sudden warmth and calm stived him, filled his consciousness with mist, and in order not to fall he grabbed his brother's shoulder, and, supported on one side by his brother and on the other by the Metropolitan, he walked up to the altar, deafened by the choir and by the carillon booming down from the belfry, and, when he saw in his brother's eyes tears of sincere brotherly sorrow and love, he could not hold back his own tears as he bowed before the goodness and simplicity of heart of the Grand Prince of Moscow.

The Cathedral of the Dormition is a terrible sight. The walls are blackened with smoke, the stucco under the paintings is cracked and in some places has fallen off. The dead lie amongst the débris, the pools of congealed blood and the horsedung, and Rublëv's ikonostasis is slowly burning out; heavy blue smoke curls up from cracks in the wood.

In one corner of the ransacked cathedral a fire has been lit, and some Tartars are heating iron rods.

In the middle of the cathedral, below the smouldering timbers of the ruined cupola, through which can be seen a pale, indifferent sky, Father Patrikei is lying, stripped to the waist, on a charred, square wooden beam. He is being tortured. The sacristan is breathing heavily, his eyes are partly closed, one lid lower than the other, his dry lips are cracked, and on his dirty neck, beneath hair sticky with sweat, a little vein is pumping convulsively.

The Tartars crouch on their haunches around the fire. They are relaxing. One young Tartar, sticking out his tongue because he is concentrating so hard, is carefully slicing, with a knife, sharp, uniform slivers from a pine plank, and sharpening them.

One of the Tartars goes up to Patrikei.

'Well, what about telling us a little more?' he addresses the priest.

'No,' replies Patrikei softly, without opening his eyes.

'But I want you to,' the Tartar grins.

'And I don't.' The sacristan opens his eyes.

'Never mind, I'll hammer some spikes under your nails and then you'll start wanting to.'

'Yes . . . if you . . . do the spikes . . . then of course . . . with spikes.'

The others come over to him from the fire.

'Maybe you'll say then, without any spikes?' the Tartar goes on.

'Say what, what do you want to know?'

'Oh dear, oh dear, what a bad steward! Forgotten, have you, where you hid the church gold!' The Tartar shakes his head.

'Of course I'm bad . . . of course I'm no good,' Patrikei agrees. 'It was from charity Father Archimandrite kept me on . . . He didn't trust me . . . Never took me into his confidence, he hid all the gold himself, I don't know . . .'

'Never mind, you'll soon find out!' The Tartar grins and gestures to the others. They all move in on Patrikei and stretch his arms along the edges of the block.

'Wait, wait . . . I'll tell you everything! I buried it, I buried all the gold, I did . . . under the fence, by the right-hand post, I did. . .'

'Ahah, come on now, we can't have that, I tell you! How much more do we have to go on digging up the earth by that right-hand post of yours, eh? Are you trying to be funny?' The Tartar can barely contain himself.

'Isn't that terrible, now,' mutters Patrikei thickly, 'it must all have been stolen! It must have been your Tartars that stole it, they're nothing but a bunch of scoundrels, your lot . . . It's yours have got it . . . you ought to be questioning them . . .'

The Tartar swears furiously in his own tongue and says something to the soldiers. They tie the sacristan's hands to the cross bar and bend over him.

Piercing shrieks echo under the vaulted roof: 'A-a-ah! Sore! Ay, Mama! It's sore . . . Ayee, Mama! Mamma, Mamma, darling!'

Patrikei's head thrashes about, the back of it beats against the log, and suddenly, with a piercing wail, he goes quiet, sighing out the word, 'Dying . . .'

The Tartar looks into his face with disgust and turns away. The Young Prince comes into the cathedral accompanied by several drunken soldiers.

The Prince goes up to the prostrate figure of Patrikei on the wooden block.

'Well, has he said anything?' he enquires, shuddering as he looks at the sacristan's mutilated hands.

'He's lying all the time, won't speak the truth at all, he won't. And now he's fainted again.'

'And what do you think you've been doing!' The Prince looks reproachfully at the Tartar and turns away to take a few steps towards the door, but is stopped by the feeble voice of the sacristan. 'Wait, wait, don't go away, Judas, Tartar scum,' he intones, and large tears trickle out from under his closed, trembling lids. 'Take a look at how these monsters are torturing a Russian, an innocent Orthodox Russian, you just look. The bandits are breaking his bones for him . . . tearing out his nails . . . look, will you, and let me look at you . . . Wait, now . . . while I come to myself, and open my eyes . . . I want to look at that filthy face of yours, your filthy, Judas, Tartar face . . .'

'Don't talk rubbish.' The Prince grins. 'I'm Russian.'

'D'you think there's any mistaking you? I recognized you by that head of yours, that Tartar, Judas head . . . You sold Rus to the Tartars . . .'

Patrikei opens his eyes with difficulty: 'I recognized you straight away . . . You mark my words, the words of an innocent victim: your cursed feet are not going to walk on Russian soil . . . I swear before the Lord God – they shall not! I shall kiss the cross!' Patrikei shudders violently, and suddenly shouts at the top of his voice, 'Give me a cross, give an Orthodox man a cross!'

'Coming up!' shouts a Tartar loudly, cheerily from beside the fire, as he pulls a white-hot cross out of the flames. 'Just wait! It's not very hot!'

The Prince, his head bowed, walks slowly along beside the wall with its mutilated paintings and, knocking open a small door, finds himself on the narrow stone staircase leading to the belfry, and all the time the same peaceful, false pictures keep crowding into his head . . .

. . . The choir was carolling, the singers' voices hovering

unimaginably high, and the candle-flames quivering in harmony with the choir's responses: '. . . let all that be round him bring presents unto him that ought to be feared: he is terrible to the kings of the earth.' – and the Younger Prince bent forward towards the heavy, gold cross, gleaming with precious stones, in the hands of the Metropolitan and, with a slow kiss, swore before the Almighty to inviolable friendship with his elder brother; and the good tears in his eyes doubled everything around him, surrounding it with a rainbow halo, as his lips touched the warm gold, and he kissed the Grand Prince three times, and the Metropolitan sealed their oath with the sign of the cross . . .

'You were shouting about a cross?' the pock-marked Tartar asks Patrikei, cheerfully narrowing his eyes and putting the white-hot, sparkling cross up to his lips. 'Go on, kiss it! That's what you wanted, isn't it?'

Patrikei looks at the cross, spluttering with heat above his face, and sees the defiled arches of the cathedral, where such a short time before he had been filled with a sense of delight and joy, where for the first time in his life he had been unable to restrain his tears, the tears of someone touched by a great and beautiful truth, as he gazed at these walls, painted by Rublëv and his comrades – now charred, unrecognizable, streaming in the searing heat from the white-hot iron held up to his face.

'Well, what were you swearing then,' the pock-marked Tartar chivvies him.

'What was I swearing,' Patrikei repeats, trying to grasp the point of the question. 'I swore . . . that . . . I swore that soon your pagan feet . . . would not be here any more! Never again! Soon all of you godless . . .'

'Why aren't you swearing?'

The Tartar brings the white-hot cross even closer to Patrikei's face, and the latter tries to escape, desperately pressing his head on to the wood of the beam on which he is lying.

'Well, scared? Are you frightened?'

'What of?'

'Dying.'

'Why would I be scared? Why would I . . . I haven't killed people, I didn't work on Sundays . . . I never betrayed the faith . . . and if

124

there are some sins, then maybe . . .' Patrikei moves his eyes from the cross to the wall.

Above him in the torrid air there quivers an angel with a trumpet, announcing the beginning of the Last Judgement. The angel stares down at him, merciful and tender . . . – 'If there are sins, he'll forgive us, the Lord is merciful, he'll forgive us . . . It's true, Lord, isn't it, you will forgive me?' Patrikei addresses the silent figures on the walls.

A long-legged black mare is led into the cathedral. Her shoes ring out disturbingly, clip-clopping over the flagstones.

'That's enough, or it's going to get cold!' The Tartar has had enough of holding out the heavy cross, and he is beginning to lose his temper.

Patrikei smiles wildly, his eyes wide with hatred: 'And you are all going to be burning in boiling pitch! All of you!' And, rejoicing in the prospect, he starts to laugh, a thin, spluttering laugh. 'You will go away, and we shall build it all again! And it will be even better than the first time! We shall all . . . and you will be in a lake of fire and brimstone with your guts pouring out!' Patrikei breaks into a high-pitched laugh, broken by tears.

The Tartar presses the cross down hard on to the priest's face, and a terrible, inhuman roar, full of pain and powerless fury, tears the emptiness of the dead cathedral.

The Tartars drag the giggling, squirming Patrikei to the entrance, and tie his feet with rawhide.

'Glory to you . . . Oh Lord!' The words can be made out in the giggle that is choking the priest. 'That you . . . have allowed the plundering and the murder . . . Now you have put such hatred into our hearts! Such strength! Thank you . . . We shall destroy them all . . . the monsters!'

The Tartars tie the other end of the rawhide to the mare's tail, and then give her glossy quarters a blow with the red-hot cross.

The mare rears, comes down on the flagstones with a crazed clatter, and dashes through the doorway, dragging behind her Father Patrikei, giggling, delirious, dying, out of the desecrated, destroyed, corpse-strewn Cathedral of the Dormition.

Vladimir is crackling and moaning from all the fires. Thick black smoke rises towards the sky, soot is carried in the wind. Tartars and

Russians are burning, slaughtering, plundering, as if there were no limit to violence, as if the bounds of human cruelty were being drawn back, further and further, out of people's reach. Weeping and groaning float above the city.

The Younger Prince climbs the belfry, up the ancient, worn stone steps, in order to be able, from the top, to weigh up, appreciate, define the full extent of his revenge, fed on hatred and on his boundless, ineradicable longing for power.

And the higher he climbs the slower time moves, the slower his heart beats, the heavier and more despairing the sweep of the Vladimir women's hands as they try to repel their loathsome, filthy, open-mouthed rapers, the more hopeless the tears and the sharper the unnatural sense of an incipient, flickering, guilt.

The prospect of Vladimir from the top of the belfry is devastating: from up here all the sobbing, moans, imploring voices, curses – can be heard more clearly than ever, the black smoke in the air hardly seems to be moving; tears as momentary as lightning hang unflowing on eyelashes, and wounds are perpetually opening up under the knife, old men are burning in inextinguishable fire, and pain and despair are crystallized for ever – as you look and listen from the very top of the Dormition bell-tower.

The Prince gazes down at the ashes and the cries, and his clear eyes, with their tiny, poppy-seed pupils, water in the wind that blows unrestricted, high above the ground.

The empty, shattered, half-burnt Cathedral of the Dormition is reminiscent of an enormous stone cavern. From above, from the yawning holes where the cupolas have been torn down, a diffuse, deadening light falls, together with a fine, cold drizzle, through the charred openings.

Andrei is on his knees beside the half-burnt ikonostasis, among the corpses. He is barely recognizable. The empty gaze from his sunken eyes wanders through space, not focusing, noticing nothing, the congealed cut on his face is black, his cassock, torn and burnt in several places is slipping off his shoulders, his right hand is wrapped in a rag, black with dried blood.

He looks as if he were intending to pray, but all at once has forgotten not only the prayer but all words. He is kneeling, frozen to the spot, alienated, like a congenital deaf-mute who has suddenly lost his sight – the only thing he had.

And then Andrei suddenly feels on his shoulder a familiar, dry, light, confident hand, and its touch evokes in his memory an infinitely distant, unbearably happy time.

'I'm glad you've come. I so wanted to talk to you.' Andrei speaks hurriedly, falling over his words.

'If you hadn't wanted me to, I should never have come,' answers the familiar, cracked voice from behind his back.

'You've arrived just in time, I haven't slept for three nights, and when I dropped off last night I was falling somewhere, and for some reason I dreamt of you, and you were looking in through the window, only not from below, but from up above somewhere, from the top of the window frame, you were hanging head down, and looking in, and wagging your finger at me, and I was in an empty hut, and there were two Mongols with me, and they were twisting my head round, and you were looking in and tapping on the window with your finger, tap! tap! And I shouted out to you . . .' Andrei breaks off suddenly and is silent.

'What did you shout?'

'Listen, what is happening?' he asks, without any connection. 'Killing and raping along with the Tartars, ransacking churches along with the Tartars, burning sacred books. Think what has been going on here.'

'But I know about all that. I know all too well.'

'When they were killing him, they tortured him appallingly, they burned him on a slow fire . . .'

Andrei speaks with agitation, fervently; he seems to be shivering.

'Who?'

'Oh, you know, him, what's his name, that relation of mine . . .'

'They've killed so many, how am I supposed to remember them all.'

Theophanes wraps his habit around him as if to keep warm and, pushing his hands into his sleeves, he leans back against the charred wall.

'Yes, and he had to kiss a cross they'd made white-hot,' Andrei goes on, agitated, 'and that's how he died, with no idea of what was going on, and he kept shouting, "You'll all be destroyed, and

127

we shall build it all up again!'' And the Tartar just laughed . . . what did it matter to him? ''You'll tear each other's throats out without any help from us!'' Can you imagine anything more shameful! When I saw the Prince himself throwing holy books on to the fire, I thought either I had gone mad, or . . .'

'And did I not tell you! And you would argue. You made my blood boil on that occasion . . .'

'Forgive me. But now I'm worse off than you, you're dead already, whereas . . .'

'Don't provoke God!' Theophanes interrupts him severely.

'That's not what I meant! What I mean is that I've spent half my life in blindness! Half my life, like that . . . It was for them, I was doing it all for other people, day in day out, night in night out. There were times when I couldn't look at daylight for three days at a stretch: my eyes were too painful. And I persuaded myself that it was a joy for them, a support for their faith. And they, these Orthodox folk, took my ikonostasis, look, they took it and burnt it. Set fire to it. Are they human beings at all!'

'What did I tell you!'

'Don't we all have one faith, and one land. And yet they took it and burnt it, they didn't think twice, and how was it that God allowed it? They were standing and watching, and one of them was even smiling. Just like that.' Andrei smiles a lifeless, terrible smile, and weeps. 'Do we not all share the same blood? They've killed them all: Foma, Piotr, Grigori, and my Sergei, too . . . That day when I found him, Seriozhka, when I found Sergei!'

'Well, that's it, time for me to go.' Theophanes frowns.

'Wait, please don't go,' mutters Andrei, hastily, afraid, sniffing through his red nose. 'What is it, can't you bear it? Is it too painful? All right, I won't go on. I don't want you to go. Let's go and sit down, and have a talk. I'll tell you . . .'

'I know it all already . . .'

'We'll go into a cell together, there's a secret one over here, I spent a week buried in there . . . We'll sit and talk . . . We'll talk till it grows dark. And all night! I'll tell you how we worked here . . .'

'I have to go.' Theophanes turns round, but Andrei stops him: 'I haven't told you the most important thing!'

Theophanes stops. Andrei plucks up his courage and says: 'That's it. I shall never paint again.'

'And why not?'

'Because nobody needs it. If I wasn't able to convince people through my art that they are people, that means I have no talent of any kind. And so I shan't ever touch an ikon or a brush or paints ever again . . . That's it . . .'

'You're wrong. Just because they've burnt your ikonastasis! Do you know how many of mine have been burnt?'

'Where?'

'In Pskov, in Novgorod, in Galich!'

'But if you were alive you wouldn't paint either. Am I not right?'

'What a sin to take upon yourself! Of course you're not right!'

'I know that the Lord is merciful, he will forgive me. I shall do penance. I shall take a vow of silence before God. I shall not speak. I have nothing left to talk to people about. Isn't that a good idea?'

'It's a bad idea,' says Theophanes sadly.

'You yourself said once, "If you can't say it then stop talking!" Don't you remember?'

'I said all sorts of things!' Theophanes sounds indignant, and after thinking for a moment, he sighs. 'I can't advise you. I have no right to give you advice. It's not possible.'

'Didn't you go to heaven?'

'What difference does it make! All I can say is that it's all quite different from what you all imagine. I must go.'

'Rus . . .' Andrei's voice trembles. 'She endures everything, this country of ours, and she will endure to the end . . . But how long is it all going to go on? Eh? Theophanes?'

'I don't know. Probably for ever.' Theophanes walks away without looking round.

It is starting to snow. The flakes fall slowly, singly, tentatively on to the floor of the cathedral. Theophanes suddenly stops beside a wall that is blackened by smoke, on which a fragment of painting has survived: a robe, part of a shoulder, a hand . . .

Putting his head on one side as old men do, he gazes intently at the painting and says: 'How beautiful it is . . .' Theophanes makes a clicking sound with his tongue and turns to Andrei, who is standing in the middle of the cathedral, head raised, hand outstretched, catching the tentatively falling snowflakes on his palm. Theophanes smiles. 'Listen, you mustn't stop, it isn't you that you're depriving of joy, it's other people. Eh?' he asks quietly.

'It's snowing,' Andrei says instead of answering. 'There is nothing more terrifying than snow falling inside a cathedral. Is there?'

No one answers. Andrei looks round the cathedral, and finding no one who might reply to him he goes outside to the street, which is starting to turn white, but because of all the charred huts, black corpses and frozen mud the oblivion of whiteness cannot prevail.

Andrei walks down the steps of the cathedral, and before he has time to go more than a few steps, the simpleton, their Vladimir innocent, comes out from behind a corner and rushes up to him. She is smiling, muttering something, burbling, either trying to tell him something interesting or else complaining. Her eyes are empty, there is no passion in her tears, and her attachment is like that of a faithful dog.

The snow is starting to fall faster. Around the next corner they suddenly come upon Sergei. He is standing in the middle of the icy road and poking his foot into a frozen puddle. Catching sight of Andrei he runs up to him, breathless with happiness, and it is clear that for the last few days he has never stopped thinking about him. Sergei tugs at him, overjoyed . . .

'I was looking for you, looking everywhere for you! Where were you, where did you . . .' He breaks off.

Andrei does not look at him, he stares straight ahead, trying not to hear, determined never again to pay any attention to human speech, and from now on to treat it as noise, as mere empty sound.

Sergei, alarmed, leaves him be, and walks along beside him, prepared for the worst that might happen.

They walk out of the gates. The broken gates that have been wrenched out by the roots.

Dusk is falling. It is snowing. Wolves are prowling in the bushes, and they howl, mournfully.

Autumn. Golden autumn. A weary sun pours warm light over the empty fields, and a gleaming spider's web moves in the mild air, catching on bushes from which leaves are scattering, on tough wayside grasses, on snicks in the time-polished beams of the monastery walls.

For several hours now, from dawn on, a tattered beggar has been hanging around the monastery gates. He has been walking slowly to and fro in front of the gateway, glancing into the courtyard, in the middle of which rises a white cathedral bathed in oblique midday sunlight, or standing for long periods by the wicket-gate, not moving, leaning on a knotted stick, or, whenever he hears voices approaching, limping hastily out of sight.

As silence falls again, he returns to the gates. His tattered rags give him no warmth, his bald head is uncovered, and an empty bag, like a symbol of humiliation and ill-luck, hangs on a string behind his back. From time to time the beggar is racked with feverish coughing, and puts a dirty palm over his mouth. It is Kirill.

A cart rolls towards the gates from the foot of the hill, pulled by an emaciated gelding and driven by a barefoot peasant. In it are several baskets filled with apples.

'Good friend, for the love of Christ give an apple to a sick man . . .' begs Kirill, his voice feeble and hoarse, almost a whisper.

'Get along now, go on,' the man sends him away impatiently. 'There's nothing to pay quit-rent with as it is. God will provide . . .'

The gate-keeper monk opens the gates and the cart rolls through.

Kirill gazes wistfully at the familiar Andronnikov Monastery, and at the new buildings and outhouses that have appeared since he left.

As he is closing the gates the monk turns to Kirill: 'Come in, man of God, and have a rest. You're surely hungry.'

Kirill steps over the threshold of the monastery with a tremulous feeling of joy and fear.

The gate-keeper leads him to the far end of the yard, where, under a sloping roof, several monks are sorting through a pile of apples, washing them and wiping off leaves. On a scrubbed table lie heaps of leaves for sousing – dill and parsley, and a mountain of blackcurrant and raspberry leaves. All around stand sweet-smelling oak tubs.

The monks are throwing the damaged and wormy apples into a basket, around which several beggars and cripples sit picking out apples and eating them greedily, paying no attention to one another.

Without a word they move up to allow Kirill to join them.

He crosses himself, mutters a hasty prayer and throws himself on the small, green apples.

'Even the apples are somehow lop-sided!' blurts out the tall monk.

'Well? Apples are apples. You should be grateful that at least they've fruited,' a fat monk with a womanish face consoles him.

'Thank you, thank you!' the tall one clowns.

'Oh, I'm so hungry, Brothers,' moans a pale, beardless novice.

'It's too early to start protesting, Nikolai.' The tall one is in a thoroughly spiteful mood. 'What sort of song and dance will you be making come the winter!'

'What d'you mean? Winter is winter . . .' says the fat one.

'I mean there'll be nothing at all to eat this winter, let alone in the spring – we'll be chewing our bast shoes! There won't even be any apples left. In all these years that the earth has been carrying me, I've never seen hunger like this!'

'We're all of us dying bit by bit, God forgive us,' blurts out the hunchbacked beggar, still chewing.

'Never mind, the Lord will see us through,' the fat monk says comfortingly. 'We have mushrooms, and onions, and we'll souse some of the apples, and dry some . . . Look how many we have.'

'It's all very well for you, Serafim, look at the paunch you've got on you, you could fast for the whole winter, but what about us bean-poles?' the tall one teases him.

'Not my fault, is it?' Serafim is offended.

'Ooh, I really am dying,' mutters the pale novice. 'I can't see straight, my head's spinning, I'm so hungry . . .'

'Here, you chew an apple, get your teeth into it. Look, I'll find you a beauty. Red and sweet. Get your teeth into that.' Serafim hands the wretched young man a fine, large apple.

'Oh, I can't even look at it, let alone . . . What do you think!' groans the novice, turning away. 'I have to go running out ten times a day, they just turn me!'

'You put up with it, now. What are you playing at, making the Lord angry about nothing. As if he hadn't enough to worry about without you. Have a chew at that and you'll feel better.'

'Stop shoving it into my face, will you, I can't bear it. I want to eat – I want meat, and bread.'

'Stop it!' Serafim is alarmed. 'You mustn't even say those words. Go on, chew it, chew it when you're told.'

The novice takes the apple, overcomes his revulsion, and bites off a small piece, which he chews for a long time, until in the end he begins to feel a kind of satisfaction.

'What an impatient fellow you are, to be sure,' observes the fat man with surprise. 'Just like some Greek, or Turk or something.'

'Why a Turk?' enquires the tall one with interest.

'They say it's only Turks who have to have everything then and there on the spot! They can't bear to wait for anything.'

'Ye-e-es, times are bad.' The hunchback sighs.

'Things are even worse in Vladimir,' hisses Kirill in a loud whisper. 'They don't even have any apples there. The Tartars burnt the lot last autumn. Pounded bark – that's what people have there.'

'Why are you whispering?' The tall monk has been staring curiously at Kirill for some time.

'I'm not whispering, I've caught a chill,' comes the answer. 'I had to spend the night in the lake.'

'Whatever for?'

'It was the wolves forced me, they were on my heels all the time. It's what hunger does to them. Even though they're scared they still come after you. So I went into the lake up to here to get away from them.' Kirill puts his hand up to his throat. 'And there I stood, and they sat down on the bank in a row, and just sat there. There I was praying to God that they wouldn't jump at me. I went on standing there till it started to grow light. Then they walked off, and I could hardly get out, I was numb all over, and now I've been shivering ever since yesterday . . .'

The unfortunate novice, after eating the apple quite unconsciously, suddenly turns green, and, pressing both hands

133

over his mouth in a burst of nausea, dashes out from under the gallery, convulsed and coughing. They all watch him in silence as he vanishes around the corner.

'So you're from Vladimir . . .' The tall man pursues the conversation as if nothing had happened.

'Well, I was just living there . . .' whispers Kirill vaguely.

'Here comes another Vladimir man.' Serafim smiles, looking into the far corner of the courtyard. 'Rublëv . . . Andrei . . . You've maybe heard of him . . .'

The beggars all stop chewing and turn quickly to look. Past the cathedral along the stone-paved path comes Rublëv. He walks evenly, his arms folded on his chest, gazing straight ahead with an air of severity, his face tense and inaccessible. Close on his heels comes the innocent, barefoot, in a loose shirt, her huge belly protruding. She is near her time.

Kirill gazes after him, open-mouthed, and in order not to betray his agitation does not even dare to swallow the saliva that has gathered in his mouth. The tall monk is staring at him, and Kirill is aware of his scrutiny.

'A bit scraggy for an ikon painter, isn't he . . .' observes the hunchback.

'He's not an ikon painter any more,' explains Serafim. 'He hasn't painted anything for a long while now.'

'Why is that?' asks one of the pilgrims.

'Why indeed! Nobody knows. He doesn't say anything. He's made a vow of silence . . . Nobody knows. He's given up ikons altogether.'

Kirill, following the conversation, is rummaging anxiously in the apple basket.

'But why did he take a vow of silence, I'd like to know?' persists one of them.

'Why do you have to go on like that? "Why, why".' Serafim is irritated.

'He must have sinned, so he's doing penance,' explains the tall one. 'You see, he's brought the simpleton with him from Vladimir, and look at her . . .' The tall man makes a gesture with both arms that suggests a large belly. 'Blessed innocent she may be, but she knows what's what, all the same.'

'He brought her here for his own shame,' concludes the

hunchback, 'so as to have his sin in front of his eyes all the time . . .'

'So much for holiness!' Serafim exclaims portentiously, with a sigh.

'That's obviously why he gave up painting. He's ashamed to touch a holy ikon,' the hunchback declares, pleased with his own ingenuity.

'And no shame before people!' One of the others sighs.

'What about his team?' wheezes Kirill, and starts coughing, bends double, his bald head turning brown with the strain. 'What about Andrei's team?' he repeats, not raising his head.

'It's collapsed, it seems,' answers Serafim. 'Some were killed by the Tartars, apparently, and the others have drifted off in different directions.'

The tall one is still scrutinizing Kirill.

'What about Daniil? He still alive?' whispers Kirill huskily.

'People say different things,' explains Serafim. 'Some say he's gone to the north, others that the Tartars took him away, and some even say he was sold as a slave to the Europeans.'

The tall monk stands up and walks over to the beggar: 'It's Kirill, isn't it? Eh?'

Kirill doesn't move, he sits there on the bench, not raising his head.

'Kirill!' exclaims the tall one loudly.

Kirill's red pate drops still lower; the beggarly figure nods rapidly in acknowledgement, and a salt tear hangs on the end of his rheumy nose.

Andrei and the pregnant simpleton, who constantly dogs his steps, walk across the monastery courtyard. They walk past the white stone walls of the cathedral, past the huge elm with its rustly leaves, as yellow as egg yokes, and into the shadow of the wooden gallery, on through it over the dead, springy earth, and down the steps into a long, gloomy corridor with tiny iron-barred windows set in its thick walls. Apples lie everywhere: on the earth in the gallery, on the floor of the corridor, and on the windowsills.

They walk on, and Andrei takes no notice of the whispering behind his back, nor of the Brothers' sidelong glances; he walks without lowering his eyes even when the whispers have grown almost into shouts, and the looks have become openly mocking.

As for the simpleton, it is all the same to her. She does not understand the mockery, nor does she see the smiles of contempt; she feels the chill autumn earth with her bare feet, greedily breathes the astringent air that smells of fallen leaves, and tries to keep up with Andrei.

In the inner yard, along the wall in which there are neither doors nor windows, stands a row of oak tubs; they are half-filled with water, and bright maple leaves float on the surface.

A little to one side glows a huge, dying bonfire, with round stones heating in it. The wind blows cautiously on the tinkling red embers, and from inside they are filled with dazzling, ineffable flame.

Andrei puts twigs on to the fire, and they twist and wriggle on the coals, crackling, merry, all of a sudden incandescent as they are seized by hot, white fire.

The simpleton keeps the fire going, gathering shavings in the yard. She cannot bend down because of her belly, and by each shaving or twig she has to crouch down on her haunches.

On the far side of the yard, from behind a wing of the monastery, comes the novice, emaciated, exhausted from vomiting; like a sick dog he keeps out of sight of other people and wants to find some quiet, isolated place. Miserable, weak, stumbling, he keeps spitting and wiping his mouth with his sleeve. Unable to stand, he sits down on a beam and, hiding his face, covered in drops of sweat, in his hands, he mutters to himself.

'Lord, my God, Almighty, just one crust . . .'

He takes his hands from his face and his eyes meet the steady gaze of Rublëv. Andrei looks down, picks up a pair of blacksmith's tongs from the ground, and walks towards the fire. Grabbing a red-hot stone with the tongs he flings it into the nearest barrel. There is a fierce hiss, the water instantly boils, and the barrel fills with steam.

Andrei returns to the fire and tries to pick out a large, heavy stone with the tongs, stirring the flaming embers and bringing down the pyramid of bluish-grey, heated stones, but the boulder slips away; the tongs clang on its smooth sides, leaving trails of sparks, the boulder darkens as it cools down, and Andrei has to thrust it into the hottest part for it to heat up again, in order to start the whole business again with fresh strength and fresh obstinacy:

carefully turning the hot stone over with the tongs, pushing the opened tongs under it because the stone is very large and it cannot be gripped properly, it can only be dragged along from below as if with a spade. Andrei, turning his face away from the heat, tries to lift the stone, but it is almost impossible because there is nothing to grip and he is obliged to take hold of the painfully hot handles almost on top of the fire. Now, leaning intently forward, he slowly raises the stone above the fire and carefully moves backwards towards the tub, barely able to control the tremor in his hands, taking one step, then another and another, and then, trying to make as few movements as possible, he turns his back on the fire and heads for the tubs which stand some ten paces away; but the distance becomes unconquerable because when Andrei approaches the tub the stone slithers off, rolls along the ground, and with a satisfied hiss comes to rest in a puddle of rain water.

And the whole thing starts all over again. Andrei's battle with the stone. The stone, like a living creature, slithers and jumps and cools . . . Andrei, almost at the end of his strength, sweating and exhausted, finally drives the red-hot boulder into the tub. There is a piercing hiss and whistle, and for a moment he is completely enveloped in a dense cloud of steam.

He sighs with relief, wipes his sweating face with his sleeve, and sets about another boulder.

In the meantime the simpleton is living her own self-contained, concentrated life. She is sticking juniper bushes into the tubs, because once they are scalded with the hot water they are so good for cleaning the slimy, mould-covered bottoms of the barrels. The innocent's round, gentle face, covered with moles, is like the face of a child which reflects, instantly and directly, all the awareness and feelings evoked by the world around it. The simpleton is natural and primitive in the way that a rainbow or a stream are natural and have one meaning, because she has a mysterious, organic connection with every phenomenon of nature – with rain, fire, or the croaking of frogs – for she herself is a fragment of nature, and of nature at its most intimate and significant moment – on the point of bringing progeny into the world . . .

Now, with a busy frown she kneels down in front of a heap of pungent, heady juniper and picks out a few bushes and crushes the springy, sapful leaves.

Then she lifts her face towards the sky and, with the same busy air, forgetting all about the juniper, she watches a flying, white spider's thread until she loses it from view; then with a preoccupied and serious look she puts both hands to her belly, opening her puffy lips and putting her head on one side, spends a moment listening to herself, her face growing radiant, and she walks away, unnoticed by Andrei, who is struggling with the last stone.

Kirill, accompanied by a few of the monks, finds the Abbot at the door of the church, as he is coming out, giving his blessing to the pilgrims.

'Father Abbot,' calls out the tall one from afar. 'Father! Kirill has come back!'

At his cry monks and parishioners come running from all directions. Kirill tries to appear calm. He kneels down in front of the Abbot and seriously, almost tragically, starts to speak in his husky, nasal whisper: 'Father, take under your wing this slave of God, good-for-nothing Kirill, who went astray.'

The Abbot smiles at him coldly.

'You went off without asking. And here you are, back again, because you didn't like it. No, Brother, nothing doing.'

Nobody expected this, least of all Kirill. He bows his head, and after a moment's silence says barely audibly: 'Lord, what have I done to deserve this . . .'

'So you're begging to be allowed back into the "den of thieves"!' the Abbot says spitefully. 'To the traders, the money-grubbers! You thought I was too old to remember, did you? Get back to where you came from. Get back into the world. There's no room for you here!'

'Don't drive me away, Father Abbot, for the sake of our Lord Jesus Christ, don't drive me away,' whispers Kirill in despair. 'There is no truth in the world, the devil has ensnared it. I cannot live in the world, I cannot go on sinning day after day. And that's the way it is in the world. There's sin and filth all around. And the poverty everywhere, dear Lord! Accept my penitence, Father, day and night I shall kiss your feet.' Kirill tries to embrace the old man's legs, but the Abbot pushes the prodigal away.

'You were ever good at talking. You won't move me to pity.'

'Oh, Father, Father! If you knew what misery I have had to bear, what evils I have endured . . .' He speaks with such pain and despair, that the watching monks feel their throats contracting. 'Even if you were to forgive me I shall never forgive myself! If you only knew what I have had to do! I have had to work with a scythe, and with a needle . . .' Kirill breaks off, tears fill his eyes, his lips tremble as he adds, 'I even had to be a mountebank . . . they made me, the godless wretches . . .'

Any moment now Kirill might burst into tears.

The Abbot suddenly turns round, and without a word walks straight down the steps and across the courtyard.

Silence ensues, and in the silence hangs Kirill's convulsive sigh.

'You are guilty not before me but before the Lord!' the Abbot suddenly shouts, pausing in the middle of the courtyard. They all start with surprise and look at him.

'Stay here. And in reparation of your sins you will write fifteen copies of the Holy Scriptures. And do one hundred prostrations a day. You can take the cell of departed Father Nikodim.' And the Abbot strides away.

'Thank you, Lord! Thank you!' Kirill bows down to the ground, whispering fussily, happily. 'Brothers, I can do everything for you . . . I've learnt everything. I'm prepared to do anything . . . I know the doctor's art and the farrier's . . . Thank you. And Father Nikodim . . .' Kirill, on his knees, is fervently crossing himself, 'may perpetual light shine upon him! I did his washing for him that day . . .'

All the corridors, lobbies and staircases of the monastery are piled with apples. Drafts of air, carrying a heady scent of apples, make doors open and shut. Kirill is walking along a passage. He comes to the cell of the late Nikodim, opens the door and stands stock-still on the threshold. In the dim, bare cell scattered with apples, the simpleton is lying on a heap of rather blighted-looking wild apples, legs apart, clutching her belly with both hands. She looks at Kirill, her eyes half-closed, and utters a plaintive, completely childlike moan. Instantly realizing what is happening, Kirill flings his bundle on the floor and dashes from the cell. He runs down the passage towards the kitchens, tearing down a piece of coarse cloth from a washing-line as he passes, and vanishes behind a corner.

Her eyes closed, the simpleton is panting heavily. She tries to find a more comfortable position, putting her weight awkwardly on to her elbows and apples go rolling over the floor.

In front of the feet of the emaciated novice, as he walks past the half-closed door of Nikodim's cell, rolls a gnarled, maggotty apple. Nikolai stops in surprise, picks up the apple, and suddenly his ears are assailed by a terrifying, heart-rending shriek.

Kirill comes running back along the corridor. The clean cloth is thrown over his shoulder, and he is carrying a steaming tub of hot water.

'Look out, Brother, let me by now, will you,' he says very fast to the startled novice, going into the cell and setting the tub down on the floor. 'We know what to do, we'll manage . . . I'm well-versed in doctoring . . .' Kirill mutters as he shuts the door firmly in the face of the dazed novice, who absently takes a bite of the apple he has just picked up and chews it mechanically as he listens to the noises coming from the cell.

The monks are crowded round the door; from within come the cries of the woman in labour. They are all affected by the excitement and anxiety that always accompany human birth or death. Nobody speaks; only occasionally they exchange whispers and glance significantly at Andrei, who is standing motionless a little way from the others, leaning back against the wall, and praying intently in silence, his eyes closed.

The shrieks start to come more rapidly, and then die away; then there is a last, shocking, pathetic scream; a moment later from behind the door come the cries of a newborn child, choking with his first gulp of living, pure, apple-laden air.

The door opens and Kirill appears on the threshold with the baby in his arms, wrapped in the homespun cloth. He looks around at the Brothers, his eyes weary and happy.

'All well, glory be to God,' he croaks, and uncovers the child. On the white cloth lies a swarthy little face with slanting black eyes. They all look in astonishment, 'Fancy that!' says one of them, embarrassed. 'A little Tartar!'

'Never!' The ones standing at the back are incredulous.

'A little Tartar, and no mistake!' affirm those standing closer.

'Well I never . . . a brigand's son!' Brother Serafim is the most disappointed of all.

'Never mind, never mind! He's our baby Tartar!' The tall monk smiles delightedly. 'A Russian Tartar baby!'

'What are you talking about! How could he be Russian?' Serafim objects.

'Of course he is!' insists the tall one. 'Who is his mother? She's Russian, isn't she? So that's it!'

Andrei pushes his way through the crowd and comes up to Kirill as he stands with the Tartar child in his arms. They all look at him with sympathy and affection, but they have a sense of guilty embarrassment.

'We shall christen him, we'll give him a Russian name,' an elderly monk says in confident, pacifying tones. 'We shall bring him up . . .'

At that moment an unfamiliar female voice with a deep, agreeable timbre is heard behind Kirill's back: 'Give him here . . . I want to look at him . . .'

It is so odd, so inexplicable, that they are frozen to the spot.

The simpleton is talking. Talking in a normal human voice, sitting on the apples and leaning against the window-sill. Through the window the last rays of the sun can be seen on the monastery wall, the gates, and, reflected in a bend in the river, the blue sky and the distant hills, covered in sparse, unleaving woods.

Kirill, nonplussed, his eyes popping out of his head, walks over to the simpleton and hands her the baby.

She sits up, settles herself more comfortably, and takes the child as deftly and easily as if she had spent her life with babies, and, still unaware of the miraculous change that has happened to her, says quietly to the monks crowded in the doorway: 'Hush . . .'

'It's a miracle!' one of them whispers, awed, and, following the lead of the Abbot who has just come in, they all go down on their knees.

'Virgin Mother of God, rejoice, Mary, full of grace . . .' the Abbot intones in a low voice, and the Brothers repeat the words after him in joyful disorder.

The simpleton looks around them all, her gaze open and comprehending, and her eyes meet those of Andrei, who is kneeling in silence among the singing monks and looking at her attentively.

She shudders, but continues to stare with intense concentration at this man whom, she is convinced, she does not know, whom she has never seen up till this moment, but whose gaze attracts her, reminds her of something, of some other times, some other life, which may not have happened at all, which she may only have seen in some bad, painful dream.

Andrei is looking at her tenderly, happily, and smiling. For the first time since his conversation with Theophanes in the ruined Cathedral of the Dormition, he is smiling . . .

'. . . blessed art thou amongst women, and blessed is the fruit of thy womb . . .' The monks' voices sound devout and solemn.

She goes on staring at Andrei, and her face is suddenly suffused with the radiance of some memory – far away, vague, and vibrant with happiness.

. . . The crazed black mare, scorched by red-hot iron, her sweating flanks gleaming, careers through a white birch grove, tangled mane flying, eyes rolling, throwing out flecks of pink foam. Each frenzied hoof-beat rings out a second time in the forest echo . . .

The gates are wide open, and beyond is a grey, misty expanse, lashed by many days of rain and overhung by low clouds heavy with water.

Three people are sitting and drinking in the wide courtyard of a peasant's house; there is a roof overhead, and the yard is strewn with clean straw. The owner of the house is a man of about sixty, still robust, and in several places his face is streaked with scars; his two guests are a craftsman with a lean, horselike face, long yellow teeth, and a wispy beard; and a young lad who is lying across the table, his head resting on his arms.

At the side, by the opposite wall, Andrei sits with his companion – a dishevelled, travel-weary monk. Andrei has aged noticeably over the last ten years, he is no longer erect, his face is darker, and white streaks have appeared in his thinning hair. The monks have laid their food out on their pack, and are quietly eating their meal, glancing at the men seated at the table and listening to their conversation.

'It's all because of the weather . . .' The householder sighs, sadly.

'What?' asks the lean man.

'Because of the weather, I said, that's why there's all that rubbish going into your soul. Pour us another . . .'

'There's none left.' The artisan pushes away the empty jug.

'Look, there's a flask hanging on the wall over there, d'you see?' the old man points to a clay flask. 'Let's have the little darling over here. My son-in-law brought it from Moscow . . .'

'It's Moscow stuff, is it . . .' The lean one takes the flask down from its nail.

'Moscow stuff it is . . . Pour some for the lad.'

'Boriska, will you take some more?' the craftsman turns to the boy. The latter shakes his head without looking up.

'Pour him some, go on,' the host insists.

There is a sudden gust of wind, and the straw on the ground is blown about the yard.

The craftsman pours beer from the flat, clay flask.

'Just the weather for a jar,' mutters the man of the house. 'Hey, your hands are trembling.'

'Yes . . . they do a bit,' agrees the lean man vaguely.

'Give it here, you're slopping half of it!' the old man takes the flask from him and pours it himself. 'Ekh . . . It's not the same blood any more. Runtish, half-Tartar. Undergrown . . . Your health!' The old man knocks back his cup with distaste.

'What d'you mean? . . . I'm all of six foot and broad to match,' says the craftsman indignantly.

'What if you are? So were we all! But you can't fell an ox with your fist, nor will they take you in the Prince's army!'

'Have you seen my brother?'

'That's not what I'm on about. None of you have the spirit, that's what I mean. Hey, come on.' He nudges the boy in the ribs. 'Drink up!'

The lad lifts his boyish, high-cheekboned face and inebriated blue eyes, drains the cup and lets his head fall back on to the table.

'Spirit . . . What spirit, what are you talking about . . .' replies the craftsman.

'What else do you think? At Kulikovo I fought in the leading division. We were all like one man. We wiped out three thousand Tartars. And we weren't even . . . we were just peasants and artisans. We saw the Prince's force retreating. Right and left, they were. And we, God help us, we stood there. And stood our ground. But now what d'you get? If one Russian meets another on the high road he'll avoid him. Ah, it's not the same . . .' He looks around for the flask and refills the cups.

The conversation breaks off, and the three sit in silence, not looking at one another.

Andrei looks at them sadly, with compassion; deep in thought, he is listening to the wind singing in the thatched roof, the horse's hooves moving on the wooden planks of the stable on the other side of the wall, and a child crying in the distance somewhere on the edge of the village.

A bedraggled, hungry bitch appears in the gateway, her belly sagging and her nipples splashed with mud. Abjectly waggling her gaunt hindquarters she cautiously approaches the table, her mournful, apologetic eyes averted as she sniffs the table legs and the floor and, finding nothing edible, curls up under the table by Boriska's feet.

'But what is a man to think, what can we do?' The craftsman suddenly starts to speak his mind. 'Look at me, for instance, I invented a clock . . .'

The old man looks at him with disbelief.

'You what?'

'I invented a clock for the tower. To measure the time and ring a bell. What are you staring like that for? I swear by the holy cross – ' the lean fellow crosses himself, 'and they made my life hell for me in the village. "Sorcerer!" they all said, "Sorcerer!" I had to run away, to the town. They burnt my hut down . . . They're black ignorant, the people are, black ignorant.'

'Black ignorant! What was I telling you?' The old man warms to his theme. 'That's just what I was saying, that they're ignorant now, good for nothing . . . That's just the trouble these days.'

'And what were they like in your day, then?' the craftsman interrupts him. 'I've heard all about that too. There was one crafts-man there, made a pair of wings for himself. The man made up his mind he was going to fly. And the whole village was chucking stones at him. Very nearly killed him. "Your time!" They were all just as ignorant, just as crass, just as backward . . . And this fellow climbed up into the bell-tower with his wings, and jumped off, and he was flying. So he proved it, didn't he. He flew . . . and he flew away altogether.'

'Where to?' the lad asks, without lifting his head.

'Well, he flew right away.'

'Where to?'

'Flew away altogether . . .' the craftsman says vaguely.

'Crashed and killed himself,' the old man says with conviction.

'Of course he didn't crash, I'm telling you the truth, he flew away.'

'And I'm telling you he crashed,' the old man repeats obstinately.

'It didn't happen at all . . .' Boriska interpolates, still without looking up.

'He crashed . . .' The old man is mocking, and sure of himself.

'He flew away.'

'Flew away-ay-ay!' the lad suddenly shouts under the table, still without lifting his head. Alarmed, the dog scuttles away from Boriska's feet, and stops in the gateway with her tail between her legs.

'He crashed,' the old man argues, drunk and aggressive.

'He flew away, it's true, he flew away.' The craftsman is tired of arguing.

'He crashed.'

'Let's have a drink,' suggests the lean man.

'That peasant was killed,' the old man maintains gloomily.

'What difference does it make!' The craftsman raises his cup and invites the old man to clink his cup in a toast. The host does not touch his cup, he wants to be certain that he won the argument.

'So he crashed?'

'All right, he crashed . . .' the inventor reassures him, and he drinks.

'There you are, you see . . . You're all the same!' The old man is triumphant. 'You're ready to deny anything for the sake of a wretched cupful!'

'Well, I don't care any more!' The craftsman smiles bitterly, wiping his moustache with his sleeve. 'I have nothing to lose! They brought some Serb in to make the clock instead of me – some fellow called Lazar. And I like a fool used to lie awake at night thinking about it. I'd thought the whole thing out.' He bends and pulls from his bag a roll of drawings and spreads the yellowing drawings out on the table. 'There! Look how good it was? You see, here's one spring, and here's the second one, and that's all . . .'

The old man stares with gummed-up eyes at the elaborate designs, and the craftsman goes on enthusiastically. 'And this wooden cog here, look . . . And they invited this Serb in my place! D'you think I mind about the money, or what? I'd have done it all for nothing, I just wanted it to be as good as possible for people . . .'

With his unsteady hand the old man pushes aside the drawings. A crust falls on to the floor under the table. The bitch grabs her booty and, with her ears flattened as if she expects to be hit, she runs off.

'But is that what people need,' says the old man disparagingly. 'A clock . . . you're no fool, as far as I can see you're even quite a clever fellow, so what the devil are you doing wasting time on that!

We can tell the time all right by the roosters. Why can't you invent
. . . well . . . why can't you invent some cannon or something . . .'

At last there is a gleam of sunshine. In one corner of the courtyard
the dog is burying a chewed scrap in a spot hidden from view; she
checks that it is well hidden and then makes her way back to the
table.

'You should invent some kind of enormous cannon, that could
drive the Tartars away once and for all. Now that would be something. Could you think up something like that?'

The craftsman shakes his head.

'Pah! And you go on with your "for the people"! All you can do is
draw sketches of springs . . . do you at least know how to mend
locks?'

'I do . . .'

'And with hands like that how is it you can mend things at all?' The
old man moves his stiff fingers and gives a mocking smile. 'As for
people . . . D'you know what they need, your people?'

Suddenly Boriska raises his head and glares at the old man, his
eyes full of hatred, and says softly: 'What right have you to speak for
other people? What d'you think you are, the Holy Ghost or something? And you never believe anybody else. What makes you better
than the rest of us? Just that you fought at Kulikovo? I tell you you're
talking a load of rubbish, it's all you ever do! You must have fought
really badly if forty years later the Tartars are still all over Rus. Maybe
if it'd been us we'd have fought much better, more fiercely. Nobody
knows. Oh, how I hate people like you. You're just as bad as my father.'

'What d'you mean, your father? Had a skinful, have you lad?' The
owner of the house, glassy-eyed, gives a good-natured snigger.

'You don't believe anybody else, not even your own! Battle of
Kulikovo! You don't even believe your children. Your own children!
My father's a caster, a master bell-caster – Nikolai, have you heard of
him?'

'Never!' The old man is astonished. 'That your father?'

'And there you go again, not believing. He knows the secret of bell
copper and he won't tell anyone what it is. The bastard even keeps it
secret from me, from his own son.'

'Boriska, you mustn't talk like that about your father . . .' The
craftsman tries to pacify the lad.

'It's nothing to do with you, so keep your nose out of it. I'd say more than that to him. I would . . . I would . . . I'd be there, with him, heart and soul, I'd work, I'd know how to cast bells, the trade would be in his son's hands. But he's so tight he won't let go of it. And he'll die without passing the secret on . . . I know he will. He'll still be holding on to it in his grave.'

'Maybe he will tell after all,' the craftsman cautiously tries to reassure him.

'Now! He's the only one. But he's like him – ' The boy nods towards the old man. 'He won't trust anyone, no one at all. But you've got to trust us, because you're all going to die and we shall be left kicking around here, we're the ones who are going to feel ashamed before God all because of you!'

'Too clever by half, you are,' grumbles the old man. 'Pint-size – but it doesn't stop you having opinions about everything.'

'What did you think, then? That we were stupider than you?' The lad smiles spitefully and suddenly breaks off.

Along the muddy road a Tartar comes riding. He has evidently come some distance, for the horse's belly is covered in mud and the rider is wearily letting himself be rocked back and forth in the saddle. The Tartar is screwing up his eyes in the sunlight and glancing around him without interest.

Now he is hidden by the wall that runs round the courtyard, but the three sitting round the table are silent for a long time, following in their minds his mournful, dreary ride along the muddy road.

'Look at that sunshine!' The craftsman is the first to break the silence.

'How old is your father then?' the old man asks the lad.

'I don't know, but he's old . . .'

A cock crows. He is answered by another, far away. A third one joins in, and soon the whole village, from end to end, rings with the sound of cocks crowing and answering. 'Anyhow, it's not the weather that makes you feel like that at all.' The craftsman turns to the old man, smiling and showing his long, overlapping teeth. 'It's just that any Russian would sooner starve than do without his bouts of dejection – and as for something to complain about – he can always find that.'

Andrei looks at the three of them. He is following their conversation.

They are sitting facing the light, leaning on the table, each reflecting in silence about something of his own; and they thrust into Andrei's perception something immensely complex, significant, vividly expressed. Revealed to him in this utterly ordinary, everyday scene is its most precious, deep-laid meaning. There under the table are the lad's legs, lying calmly, shoeless, the left slightly extended, the right crooked, relaxed, at ease; faded hose with ragged edges just cover the slender sunburnt ankles . . .

. . . The coarsely stitched edge of the open shirt shows a finely moulded shoulder-blade and a long neck, with the head inclined . . .

'As for Germans, now, they're no good at all with low spirits. And if ever they start to feel dejected, they think they're ill,' the craftsman declares thoughtfully.

. . . The long shirt, coming below the knee, falls in straight, tranquil folds; then the old man turns, the calm is shattered, replaced by sharp, broken lines like crushed tin, colliding, ready to disintegrate; but their owner wipes his hand on the hempen cloth and the broken lines that were fixed for a moment are dispersed.

'Well, let's have a drink, and hope the Lord will give us everything in the world . . .'

Andrei gazes at them, shaken by the idea that has suddenly overwhelmed him as a complete, assimilated, harmonious design.

. . . The folds run upwards and burst out by the elbow, then vanish altogether to fall a moment later in translucent shadows from the round, robust shoulder, whence a smooth, perfect line runs down to the hand that is stretched towards the cup . . .

'It's obviously my lot – having to put up with it . . . If it weren't for my mother I'd have run away long ago . . .' The lad sighs.

Mechanically, Andrei picks up some charcoal from the floor and crumbles it in his trembling fingers, transferring it from one hand to the other, his eyes running intently over the contours of arms and shoulders as they rise gently, swiftly, flashing where the nap catches the light and then falling again with a sudden, sharp break at the elbow and vanishing in shadow between the table and the long palm.

Andrei cannot sit there on the floor any longer, and he stands up.

The three are sitting in peaceful, loving companionship, balancing one another, flowing one into the other, motionless in their wise contemplation, and the bright rays of the sun are entwined in the boy's tangled hair to form a golden halo . . .

Andrei gives a convulsive sigh and walks out from under the shelter towards the gleaming whiteness of the clean, limewashed wall of the yard. For a while he stands by the wall, his wide eyes running over its smooth alluring surface, and the charcoal dust trickles out from between his feverishly clenched fingers. Then he suddenly turns and sits down on a log and wipes his wet forehead, streaking his face with charcoal.

Close by, the hungry bitch is burying her latest booty against a rainy day, for her pups. Over the village as it lies drying in the sun, the cocks, near and far, call and answer.

'Lord . . .' whispers Andrei inside his head.

Once more the sun goes behind a cloud and the dazzling wall is extinguished, grows grey, and everything around him becomes dull and flat.

On and on speeds the raven-black mare, her headlong, tireless gallop grows ever more frenzied, her hoof-beats sound ever more alarmed, ever more frightening, and behind her in the dazzling sunlight the forest dissolves into indistinct strips, shot through by shining arrows which flash in her crazed eyes, and her flight is almost airborn.

12 The Plague: Spring 1422

Through a Rus laid waste by Tartars, internecine war, famine and plague walks a figure in a tattered cassock, so worn that it is glossy. He is sick, and exhausted by his unending journey. And his sickness is the plague that has wrapped its black breath around the vast lands of Russia.

It is April. The first, joyful, beggarly sun is coming to life in the liquescent crystals of spring snow. His feet never dry out.

In the evenings it is shivery and sinister among the black, damp trees looming through the mist that gnaws away at the snow.

The monk's face is dark and dried like a wooden idol. For a long time he has been walking along flooded roads, avoiding the villages weary from plague and famine, where people move slowly as if bemused, afraid of spilling what little remains of their dwindling life force.

The traveller arrives at the River Iauza. Sharp reports like cannon fire ring out over the breaking ice. The ice piles up in whirlpools of black water and sharp, disintegrating fragments, clear as glass.

At the water's edge the monk breaks off a long stick, and, without hesitating, he strides out on to the moving surface of the river. Exhausted and weak, risking his life, he jumps with obstinate assurance from floe to floe, coming closer with each step to the opposite bank. The current is carrying him further and further downstream towards the walls of the Andronnikov Monastery, standing black on the high bank of the river.

Through the low cell window can be seen the monastery courtyard, densely packed with smoking fires. From here the mournful figures of the monks on the grey snow, worn down with fog and smoke, look like ruffled black birds.

A low, husky, monotonous voice sounds in the stillness, and when it falls silent the wind can be heard whistling in different keys, blowing out of the cell the last of the warmth, which streams away under the door together with the acrid smoke fumigating the monastery.

'. . . in the morning sow thy seed . . .' the voice is slow and punctilious, 'and in the eve-ning withh-o-old not th-y h-a-and, f-o-or th-ou kno-owest not wh-ether shall pr-osper, either this or th-at, or whether th-ey both shall be ali-ike g-ood.'

Two sledges are sliding over the courtyard towards the gates, carrying coffins – two who have died of the plague are being carried away, and the monks are putting their belongings on to the fires with long hooks; the flames, choking with eagerness, lick the damp, worn-out cassocks, thrust their red tongues into the old, down-at-heel bast slippers squirming on the fire as if they were alive, and dense, heavy smoke spreads over the thawing snow-drifts.

'. . . Truly the light is sweet and a pleasant thing it is for the eyes to behold the sun . . .'

Bent over a table strewn with manuscripts, piles of clean parchment and written pages, Kirill is copying out the Holy Scriptures. The long years of penance have taken their toll. His head is bowed down right over the page, his eyes are screwed up, he is frowning painfully, as he gazes at what he has written.

'. . . But if a man live many years,' Kirill dictates to himself by heart, 'and rejoice in them all, yet let him remember the days of darkness; for they shall be many. All that cometh is vanity!'

Through the partially opened gates squeezes the unknown monk, soaked to the waist and in the last stages of exhaustion after crossing the river by the ice-floes. He can barely put one foot in front of the other, in his bast shoes, swollen with water.

Going up to Sergei, who is busy by the fires with the other monks, he asks him something, and then Sergei takes his arm and the two vanish round a corner.

'. . . Rejoice, O young man, in thy youth, and let thy heart cheer thee in the days of thy youth, and walk in the ways of thine heart, and in the sight of thine eyes . . .' comes Kirill's voice.

Sergei leads the traveller to Rublëv's cell and says severely: 'This is where he lives, only he is surely praying. Wait . . .' He peers through a crack in the door, which is not quite shut. 'Yes, he is praying. You'll have to wait . . .'

When Sergei walks away the newcomer goes up to the door and

looks into the cell, and he sees in one corner, in front of the ikons, Andrei kneeling, crossing himself in silence, and ceaselessly, steadily prostrating himself.

At the end of the corridor appears the figure of a monk, carrying in his hands a tin tray with herbs smoking in the corners – the monastery is constantly being fumigated. He walks past the newcomer, throws him a suspicious glance, covers him with bitter, noxious smoke, and disappears into the darkness of the corridor.

Andrei goes on and on prostrating himself, touching the cold, unplaned floor with his forehead, and his whole appearance, the fervently pressed lips, the face, dark and dessicated from fasting, the eyes, burning with a feverish glow, and above all this monotonous, consciously enforced repetition of one and the same movement, which gradually loses its meaning as a result of being repeated over and over again, suggests something that is not alive, something frightening.

Andrei rises from his knees with effort, and straightens his stiff back. His breath comes in gasps, the blood is pounding dully in his head, his face is pouring with sweat. With trembling hands he sets straight his cowl which had fallen to one side and rubs both his hands over his face. Glancing quickly at the ikonostasis he goes out into the corridor.

Opposite the door, on the stairs leading to the attic, sits the shivering monk, leaning his head against the bannisters, his eyes closed. At his feet is a puddle of water from his wet cassock and shoes.

Hearing the creak of the door he jumps to his feet and bows awkwardly.

'Abbot Nikon sent me to you, Father . . .' he blurts out in a hoarse voice.

Andrei looks at the messenger in surprise, and somewhat sternly. The latter has great difficulty in continuing.

'From the Monastery of the Holy Trinity, Abbot Nikon, . . . You know him . . . He said to tell you . . . That he's planning to build a stone cathedral there in place of the one burnt down by the Tartars . . . He has already arranged with the craftsmen . . . Master craftsmen . . . from Pskov . . . The guild . . .'

Andrei makes a gesture of impatience, and the messenger hastily tries to finish what he has to say, vehemently, losing his thread, as if afraid he will be interrupted: 'They're going to build a Cathedral of the Trinity . . . in white stone . . . A great labour . . . They've started bringing the stone over . . . really clean stone, it is, white! Father Nikon sent to fetch you . . . told me to ask you, to beg you, to paint the cathedral . . . Here, he sent this letter – ' the monk anxiously feels around inside his cassock on his chest, pulls out a crumpled, rolled-up letter, and offers it to Andrei – 'read it, please, be so good, I have been told to wait for your answer . . .'

The monk's face is burning, and there is a black, congealed crust on his cracked lips. Andrei is breathing heavily, and occasional drops of sweat run down his sunken cheeks. And so they stand facing each other in silence until finally Andrei turns and walks away along the passage.

The messenger barely manages to catch up with him, he unrolls the letter as he walks and hurriedly, breathlessly, in a voice that keeps breaking off from sheer exhaustion, he proceeds to read it to Andrei.

The grace of our Lord God and our Saviour Jesus Christ be with you, who are devoted to the Holy Trinity, the Father, the Son and the Holy Ghost.

Andrei, are you still alive?

This is too dark an hour for all Rus, the tribulations of all Orthodox folk, sent by the Lord in redemption of our sins, are too fearful, for our quarrels and arguments to be remembered. And therefore I do not remember any grudge against you, I have no word of judgement for you, and I am writing as to my brother in faith and by blood.

Terrible times have come for Rus, Brother Andrei, plague, and Tartars, and brother fighting brother. Truly, even folk at liberty these days are no better off than those who have been buried. In every corner of our land are sobbing and weeping, everywhere is dire distress! . . .

The monastery is deserted. In the middle of the bare cells of those Brothers whom the plague has carried off, trivets with bitter herbs send up laminated clouds of aromatic smoke.

Andrei quickens his step, but the desperate messenger keeps up with him, even though as he walks along in the half-darkness of the corridors and lobbies it is hard to make out the letter written in Nikon's aged hand.

. . . and so, my Brother, as you know yourself, faith in the power of our Orthodox Church has no firm foundations amongst the people. In truth, I shall not be lying if I tell you that many do not believe at all that a kingdom of truth and goodness will come about in Russia in the end . . .

The monk is convulsed with coughing and only with enormous effort does he manage to control it, before going on despondently:

. . . and I cannot give way to the devil, I cannot hand the people over into his hands, and therefore I have decided, to the glory of our Holy Orthodox Church and to the glory of our teacher Sergei Radonezhsky, to build the Cathedral of the Trinity, in stone, adorned with rich and felicitous paintings.

I appeal to your reason, your heart and your faith! Come back to the Trinity, paint the cathedral however you will, I entrust myself to you and your skill, myself and my thoughts. Believe me that I wish for you all that I wish for myself: God is merciful. He will forgive you your violation of your oath, so dear to Him will be the great aims which guide you.

If, even now, you still think evil of me and consider that I am preoccupied with worldly, mercenary matters – that is your affair. All that I told you then remains true today. Before God I am pure – I have not spent one farthing of peasants' money on myself! Nor is it for the gratification of my eyes that I enjoin you to paint the cathedral.

Peace be with you, Brother Andrei, and if you have anything against me, I beg you to forgive me, forgive me any offence I may have done you.
Nikon

The monk overtakes Andrei and falls down on the floor in front of him. His eyes glisten feverishly in the darkness: 'I entreat you, Father . . . Come back for the sake of Christ our Lord . . . They've brought the stone already . . . white stone, the whitest . . .' the messenger croaks.

Kirill moves away from the table and towards the door, and overhears a desperate, bronchitic voice carried down the corridor: 'The Abbot is old now . . . really . . . frail . . . When he was writing to you then, he was in tears, like a little child . . . Told me I must not return without your agreement . . . But I shan't be returning whatever happens . . . The Lord is going to take me . . . I am ill, it seems

. . . only I implore you . . .' The monk's strength is leaving him, he drops his head down on to his hands and goes on speaking, into the floor: 'Come, Andrei, and paint the cathedral in the name of Our Lord Jesus Christ . . . If you don't . . . then there'll be nothing . . .'

With an effort the monk raises his head and sees the empty corridor and the grey-blue smoke curling out from dead cells. And Andrei is not there.

Kirill stands, stooped, by the window. He is gazing out into the courtyard where, with a long hook in his hands, the mute Andrei Rublëv is busy with a fire of smouldering rags.

For a long time he stands there by the window, motionless, staring at one spot. Then he purses his lips, and, wrapping his cassock around him as if he were cold, almost runs from the cell and walks quickly down the smoke-filled passage.

In early summer, along an even, well-beaten road stretching out over an endless ploughed plain, five blind men are walking in single file. Four of them are craftsmen who were once blinded by the Grand Prince. In front, behind the shock-headed lad who is their guide, walks the master – now an old man bowed with years, behind him, holding on to the edge of his shirt, comes the erstwhile carver, Mitiai the stammerer, after Mitiai – his brother, and, holding on to the latter's staff, an unfamiliar young man with cloudy, immobile eyes. Last of all comes Gleb, who once appropriated a scrap of Rublëv's azure.

There is nothing to relieve the dreary, long, melancholy road.

'Mishka, where are we?' asks the master.

'On the road . . .' answers the guide grudgingly.

'What road? "On the road" . . .'

'Just on the road, on the hard road . . .' Mishka doesn't feel like telling him anything.

'Can't you tell me properly? Or have you forgotten how to talk straight?' the master says crossly.

'Well, it's a long, straight road . . . a hard road . . .' the lad goes on obstinately.

'That all?'

'What else d'you want?'

'You mean we're walking along somewhere where there's nothing at all?'

'Nothing at all,' replies the guide confidently.

'You're always talking rubbish.' Gleb gives a disparaging laugh.

'All right, so it's rubbish,' the boy agrees spitefully. 'There's a river on the left.'

'What river?' The blind men liven up, smiles appear on their faces.

Impulsively, the guide starts to invent: 'A deep river, deep and slow-flowing, and on the other bank ... Oh, think what's on the other bank!'

'What, what? What is it?' several impatient voices say at once.

'What is it?' The lad grins. 'Bushes.'

The master walks straight on, raising his head, and his imagination paints a quiet, narrow river that he saw once long ago, in his childhood, covered with water-lilies, with tall grey willows on the far bank, and a little path leading uphill, along which a woman is walking with two buckets of water on her yoke, in a coarse, multi-coloured sarafan, and the banks of the river are overgrown with bushes interwoven with hops ...

Mitiai, smiling, walks head down, and as if from the edge of a high precipice he sees a great, deep river, with a long, thickly wooded island in the middle, above it rises the smoke from campfires, and leaden ripples cover the water where the river winds round the low bank on the opposite shore, where the village stands, gripped by smoke and flame ...

But Mitiai's brother does not see any river ... He sees a girl in tears standing on a path among young pine trees hung with luminously gleaming forest gossamer, showing them the way to Zvenigorod, and the tears are pouring down her face, and he walks away with the others, on and on, and she becomes smaller and smaller, then there is a sudden bend in the road and the weeping girl vanishes behind the trees ...

And the young man with white, blind eyes sees ... All he sees is perpetual black space, teeming with sounds and smells, and filled with an untold number of invisible and indescribable objects, planes and masses. He has been blind from birth.

Gleb is walking at the rear with his head back, remembering a dazzling, clear, fast-flowing river, so clear that its pebbly bed looks completely white, and the bushes, black against the sandy, sloping bank on the far side, down which a herd of horses is making its way through the willow bushes towards the river; the first to walk into the water is a foal, who sets his legs wide apart and drinks greedily, lifting his head from time to time and dropping heavy, sunlit drips into the icy water . . .

'Why don't we go down to the river and have a swim?' suggests Gleb.

'Ah, but it's hardly a river . . . you couldn't swim here. It's really more of a bog . . .' The lad tries to extricate himself.

The shining river with the foal is replaced in Gleb's imagination by a flat, steamy swamp, dotted with tufts, with huge black firs around the edge. The sun can hardly push away the heavy, grey mist . . .

'And on the bog! Look at that!' By now the boy is really carried away, and his voice is jubilant: 'There's a tree . . .'

. . . Gleb can see a solitary, crooked tree standing in the middle of the swamp . . .

'And on the tree!' – the guide throws discretion to the winds – 'there's a bird . . . with a human head!'

He receives a sharp blow on the ear with a stick. They all stop, and the old man, trembling with fury, exclaims: 'What are you up to, you scoundrel? Are you mocking us? Eh?'

The boy walks off a few steps, rubbing dirty tears over his face, and immediately becomes inaccessible.

'You son of a bitch, you! Eh?! Thought you'd tell stories, did you!' The old man seethes.

The lad does not answer. He is as quiet as a mouse, holding his breath and swallowing his tears, staring reproachfully at the blind men.

The master breaks off, listens, and his face falls.

'Mikhail! Mishka!' he shouts anxiously, stretching his neck.

Mishka stands close by and says nothing.

'Mikhai-ail!' cries Gleb desperately, 'Mishka-a-a!'

The blind men turn their heads this way and that and look utterly helpless and pathetic.

'Mishenk-a-a!'

'What's the matter with you all . . .' the guide gives in . . . 'I'm here . . .'

He goes up to the blind men, who fuss around, knocking with their sticks, and exchange agitated words as they arrange themselves in a file. The guide puts himself at their head, and the blind men walk on along the smooth, straight road surrounded by the dreary Russian plain.

'All right,' mutters Mishka, 'I shall run away from you all the same . . .'

Kirill walks out into the courtyard among the bonfires. The dank, heavy air presses the black smoke down on to the ground. Andrei is standing by the wall, beside the farthest fire. Kirill goes up to him and starts to speak, stuttering and hurrying: 'You know what's happened, Andrei . . . I've been thinking all this time . . .' Kirill takes a hold of himself and, mastering his agitation, goes on: 'I decided I must tell you, tell you here and now . . .'

Andrei hooks up a heavy cassock and lays it on the bonfire. The damp material covers the fire, and thick white smoke starts to pour out through the holes.

'You know yourself how I envied you,' continues Kirill, 'I was being eaten up by it, it was fearful . . . It was as if there were some sort of poison rising up in me all the time . . . I couldn't bear it any longer, that was why I left. I went off because of you. And when I came back and heard that you had given up painting, I was beside myself with joy! I spent ten years rejoicing over your unhappiness . . . And then I more or less forgot about it. I hardly cared any more, all that mattered was that I should have time to copy out the Holy Scriptures before I died.'

The glowing cassock on the bonfire suddenly bursts into tall orange flames.

'But anyhow, why am I being so contrite,' Kirill says angrily. 'I have no call for contrition as far as you are concerned, you yourself are such a sinner, far more than I am. Yes, yes, more than I am!' he repeats emphatically as he catches Andrei's eye. He is shaking as if in a fever. 'What am I! I'm an insignificant worm, I am nothing! And nothing is asked of me. But you . . .' Kirill is boiling with rage, he glares at Andrei with loathing and fury through the film of smoke and the dull tongues of flame, 'what saintly deeds did you do to be given your talent by God, what merit did you have? None! It was free! And if you didn't earn it, then you have no right to dispose of it. You have no right!'

He stumbles suddenly, flags, presses his palms against his temples: 'But that's not what I meant . . . I don't know.'

Andrei hooks up a bundle of rags and throws it on to the fire.

'I heard all that today, Andrei . . . Why can't you have some pity . . . look what fear is stalking Rus, what distress and misery people are suffering. I know! I've seen it! And I've seen your painting. Almighty God!' Kirill presses his hands against his chest, and his eyes fill with tears. 'Think of your angel – with the trumpet! People stand there gazing at it, they gaze and weep and don't even wipe their tears because they don't notice . . . Do you imagine it was easy for them to clean all the smoke and ash off your paintings and restore them? When I stood there, beggar and tramp that I was, my sinful heart was filled with light . . . God was guiding your hand, Andrei, and you . . . ' – Kirill goes closer to him and whispers in a passion: 'Never mind that I'm a sinner – listen to me: go to the Trinity and paint and paint and paint and paint! Not for Nikon, obviously it's not for him. Of course, Nikon is a renegade, a trader. Go on: don't take that grave sin on to your soul. And what a terrible sin – to refuse the divine spark. If Theophanes were alive he'd tell you the same, he'd tell you it is a great sin! Well, isn't it? Well?' Andrei looks at Kirill for a few moments, alarmed, and then averts his eyes. Kirill persists: 'Look at me, look at me, I have no talent. I shall die and there will be nothing left that is mine. God grant at least that the Scriptures will have been written out. And you don't have that much time left either, you'll die, and then you'll be sorry. Well? Do you want to take it with you to the grave? Say something won't you! Go on! Why won't you talk?'

Kirill tugs impatiently at Andrei's sleeve.

'Go on, curse me if you want! Curse me! Only don't stand there saying nothing. It was I who denounced the buffoon! It was I! Do you hear? Why won't you talk?'

Andrei is looking through Kirill with steady, frightened eyes, then he turns away, and suddenly Kirill sees on his face a strange, alienated smile . . .

. . . A sweating black horse gallops across a bridge over a stream, sweeps up the high bank, rears, baring her teeth, and with a

shake of her head careers down the steep slope, throwing up sand
and making a cloud of dust . . .

Nikon's messenger, stumbling and falling and growing weaker all
the time makes his way down to the roaring river. He has no
strength left to go on, and he sits down on the wet snow, holding
on to the trunk of a tree.

Broken ice goes rushing past him.

The bank is dotted with people watching the ice-floes. Sick
people, as weak as flies in spring, sit or stand.

And suddenly a great ice-floe comes into view, swept along by
the current, with a drunken peasant lying on it, his fur coat flung
open, his eyes closed, and he is singing a cheerful, bawdy song.

The river carries the floe further and further, until the cheerful
peasant is hidden from view by the next bend.

13 The Bell: Spring, Summer, Autumn, Winter, Spring, 1423–4

The sky, cold and pale, is mirrored in a clear March puddle lying by the doorway of a sagging hut. Towards evening there will be a touch of frost, and even the first star will not have time to see itself reflected, for a matt, fragile film of ice will be drawn across the blue water. That is, of course, if no one comes out of the hut and stumbles into it in the dark. Then there will be a gentle crunch, and on the dark, disturbed surface, along with splinters of ice, the reflection of that first star will rock for a little, then gradually grow still, as if frozen into the fresh sheet of ice spreading over the thick, cold water.

The cramped yard is piled with snow, dung and straw. By a post which leans over obliquely a gangling, skinny boy is at work. He is trying without success to hang one half of the rotting gate on to its hinge. This is Boriska, the son of the master bell-caster. He is as angular and restless as he was a few years back, only now his thin face with its high cheekbones has grown a light, colourless down.

He braces himself and tugs the warped, delapidated gate off the ground, sets it upright, and attempts to hang it on the shaky post. The thick, roughly fixed beams are heavy and unmanageable. The gate slips off the hinge, slams noisily to the ground, and splashes biting, icy slush over four horsemen in the Grand Prince's uniform who ride up to the gate from the street.

The startled horses throw up their heads, and stop in the gateway.

'Is this the right house for Nikolka the bell-caster?' asks the senior man, wiping the splashes from his face with his cap.

'It is,' answers the boy, perplexed.

'Your father, is he?'

'He is.' The lad's slanting, light eyes are wary.

'Well, go on, call him.'

'He's not there.' The boy goes back to the heavy, sodden gate.

'Where is he?'

'Dead,' the voice comes from under the creaking gate as it comes up from the ground, 'the pestilence took them all: my mother and my sisters. And my father too.'

The horseman stares at the gate behind which Boriska is struggling, and clearing his throat asks: 'Er . . . what about Gavrila the caster, is his hut near here?'

'Gavrila?' The boy's face, with a curious smile, appears from behind the grey planks. 'Gavrila's dead as well. And Kassian, the master, he died too, and Ivashka was taken away by the Tartars last year. Only Fiodor is still left, you go to him. The fifth house along . . .'

The horsemen look at Boriska in silence. The horses snort loudly, chinking their bits in their mouths, and moving their weight from hoof to hoof, making a satisfying squelch in the freezing mud.

The lad suddenly smiles impudently, showing his pale gums with short, even teeth. 'Only you'd better hurry, squires, you can hear him rattling already, that Fiodor. He's not opening his eyes, he might be taken at any moment.'

The horsemen stare in silence at their leader.

'What a time to be living in, with no one who can cast a bell . . .' the latter mutters through his teeth, without looking at them, as he turns his horse.

The lad jumps as if he has been stung by a bee, and dashes off after the horsemen. The gate that he left standing falls to the ground with a loud splash. Boriska trots along beside the horsemen.

'Hey, take me with you! Let me cast the bell. Take me to the Prince, will you?' he asks the senior man, panting and hanging on to his stirrup.

The latter, without stopping and without even looking round, says, 'Are you off your head, lad?'

Liquid flecks of half-thawed snow fly from under the hooves of the trotting horses.

'No . . . truthfully, I . . . I shall do a fine job for you . . . Anyhow, you won't find anyone else, they've all . . . all died off . . . You won't find anybody better than me!'

'Go on, lad, go on, off you go, leave us be!'

'But you won't find anyone else . . .'

'Away you go, stop getting under my feet,' says the leader angrily.

The boy stops at the edge of the trading suburb, and shouts breathlessly after the departing riders: 'All right then. So much the worse for you! I know the secret of bell-casting, and I shan't tell you!'

He sees the riders stop a little way off, and hears the senior man shout: 'What?'

'I know the secret!' Boriska is shouting at the top of his voice. 'My father knew the secret of bell copper, and he told it to me when he was dying . . . Nobody . . . nobody else knows it . . .' He wipes his flushed face, watches the horsemen conferring, and yells: 'I'm the only one who knows. My father was dying and he told me the whole secret . . .'

'What's your name?'

'Boriska!'

'Come here then!' shouts the senior man, and the lad runs towards the horsemen as fast as his legs will carry him.

The snows have gone and the spring waters have abated. Moscow River has fallen back within its banks, leaving on the bushes, and on the lower branches of the trees, dead twigs brought down by the spate and dry bundles of last year's grass, which look like devastated birds' nests. The tender, sticky green of the trees moves in the warm breeze, gleaming in the sun.

On a steep hillside where a few early flowers are already in bloom, Boriska is walking with a number of craftsmen. Behind them stride peasants with spades on their shoulders, who are to do the digging. Boriska walks ahead, feeling the suspicious, searching eyes of the artisans upon him, and concentrating on an inexplicable but clear inner voice, which he himself is barely able to make out, telling him how he should behave in the face of difficulty.

Suddenly, beneath a tall, crooked poplar, he stops. The craftsmen surround him in silence and look around.

'This is where we dig,' decides the boy.

'We can do,' agrees the eldest of the craftsmen, with a thick, greying beard. 'Only the nearer the bell-tower, the better. Otherwise, look how far we're going to have to drag it.'

Boriska, at great pains to conceal his own lack of confidence, stares in front of his feet, and either affirms or asks: 'But we can cast the bell here, too . . .'

'We can, surely . . .'

'So this is where we shall have it,' concludes the lad firmly, and beckons to an ungainly red-haired boy who is hovering around the craftsmen, evidently an apprentice. 'Andreika!'

The redhead comes running up. Boriska whispers something in his ear and gestures violently. Andreika nods, full of willingness, making it clear that he understands everything without being told. The men exchange sceptical glances.

The redhead, burning with eagerness, can hardly wait for the end of Boriska's instructions before dashing off towards the white Kremlin wall on top of the hill. The craftsmen stand in silence, their hands on their stomachs, and stare expectantly at Boriska. There is an awkward pause. Then the lad purses his lips angrily and issues an order to the peasants: 'Go ahead, measure it out!'

The peasants readily set about marking out the enormous pit. Boriska helps them, as if he were an ancillary. He drives in a peg with a wooden mallet, ties twine to it, walks away, unwinding the heavy ball of twine, and pacing out the distance, and then drives in a second peg. The pegs, freshly made out of damp, fragile alder, splinter, bend, slip away from under the mallet as if they were alive. At last the site is marked out.

The diggers prepare for work. They cross themselves, spit on their hands, and take up their spades. Boriska runs around in a state of agitation, but there is nothing he can do to help: there are not enough spades. He shades his eyes with his hand and looks impatiently in the direction of the Kremlin wall, but there is no sign of Andreika. He cannot contain himself, and going over to a short, broad peasant he grabs the spade from him.

'Let me.'

'Wait a minute, now . . .' the peasant says quietly, as if offended.

Easily, almost without effort, like a knife into lard, the sharp spades slip into the earth, the roots of grasses crunch as they are cut through, tiny pebbles polish the metal; with a gasp, a layer of fresh earth breaks away, covered in young grass, with two miniature dandelions, a whole world inhabited with ants, little insects, pink worms, ladybirds, it lies on the spade, heavy, warm, aromatic like bread straight from the oven, then slides off as it is thrown to one side and goes hurtling, hopping, down the soft slope, faster and faster, the dandelions flashing like minute yellow fires. Shedding sand and pebbles it springs down and down, growing lighter and lighter and more dishevelled, brushing noisily through the bushes and stopping in surprise as it rolls out on to the part of the hill that slopes gently down to the damp, sandy bend of road that leads, beyond the next hill, to a glistening ford over the River Moscow.

Boriska digs passionately, selflessly, with unflagging impetus, intoxicated by the earth, his spade crunches through the turf, he is filled with an overwhelming urge to dig up the entire slope, the entire field, the entire bank, and over there as well, on the other side of the river. The entire earth!

The labourers work circumspectly, with enjoyment, and glance with astonishment at Boriska, their superior, when he pauses for a moment to recover his breath, wipe away the sweat that is pouring into his eyes, and brush away the horse-flies.

The master casters look on with disapproval, exchanging remarks, and some of them are even laughing at him, impudently and provocatively.

Andreika comes running down the hillside with an armful of spades. He runs up and drops them at Boriska's feet. The latter looks up, smiling, his face pale and sweating, and turns to the master craftsmen.

'Why don't we all dig together?'

The old man rewards Andreika with a box on the ear for coming back, and says in as gentle a voice as he can manage: 'But we're not labourers. We are casters. We can't start messing around with earth.'

Boriska looks around with a conspiratorial air and says in a low voice: 'You know what my father told me before he died? He said that all casters ought to dig the casting pit themselves. I've only understood that now, in my old age, he said. That's what he told me; and then he died . . . Do you understand?'

'I don't know . . . I don't know what Nikolai said, only I am not going to start digging. When you need us, give us a shout!' concludes the old man, and walks off towards the Kremlin road, together with the other artisans.

'All right, then!' Boriska shouts after them acidly. 'I'll do your digging for you.'

Evening is falling. The men working in the pit can no longer be seen, only lumps of earth, thrown up to the top, scatter on the grass with a heavy, rustling sound.

They are all dog-tired, but no one wants to be the first to give up as they watch their superior, an undergrown boy, impetuously flinging up the earth.

Boriska suddenly notices, on a level with his face, a thick, curved root protruding out of the wall of the pit. He puts out his hand and tries to tug it out of the ground. There is a shower of earth, the root turns out to be long and pliant, with a great number of offshoots. Boriska, intrigued, walks around the wall, struggling to pull the endless pink root out of the earth, with all its knots and weird excrescences. The lad tugs at it, but it will not give any further, and Boriska's efforts are in vain. He picks up his spade and is about to cut it through, when his eyes start following it upwards, and he sees immediately above him the great, rough trunk of a mighty poplar, stretching out in all directions, its crooked grey branches covered in the first pale leaves and hung with tiny red ear-rings.

Boriska drops the root, wipes his hands on his shirt, and takes up his spade.

The group of casters make their way down the steep, well-beaten entrance to the clay quarry. Boriska hurries ahead, with a kind of ungainly, bobbing gait. Then he stops, bends down, with his hands on his knees, gazing in front of his feet. The craftsmen crowd around him. The boy picks up a lump of clay from the ground, and examines it carefully. Thrusting his long, thin fingers into the clay he brings it up closely to his face, then closes his eyes and rubs it through his fingers, like a blind man.

The old, grey-bearded craftsman looks on with mistrust and curiosity.

Boriska throws the lump of clay aside with disgust and hurries on down. The craftsmen follow him, exchanging blank glances.

At the bottom of the quarry Boriska again picks up a lump of clay, squeezes it, examines it, rubs the clay between his fingers, then throws it down and, wiping his hands on his trousers, blurts out: 'No, it's not right. It's the wrong clay!'

'We've always taken it from here in the past,' objects the old man.

'Well, you were fools to take it from here. Andreika, isn't this clay wrong?' Boriska asks angrily.

'Course it is!' agrees Andreika, delighted. The old man, offended, lowers his head in impotent anger.

'You see?' The lad turns to them. 'We're going to go on looking. Till we find what we need.'

Three figures are walking over the empty, russet, bristling stubble: Boriska, the caster with the bald head, and Andreika. They all look upset and cross.

'Listen, Stepan, maybe there's no point in doing this?' Boriska turns to the bald man.

'Of course there's no point.' The craftsman, worn out, sighs heavily. 'Look what good clay we've found. Eh? Take a proper look at it.' From inside his shirt he pulls out a lump of clay wrapped in a rag and unrolls it. 'We've put so much work into it. We found a new place. And you . . .'

'But it's not right, it's not right, can't you understand!' shouts Boriska in desperation.

'You keep on and on! It's the end of August, and we still haven't dug the clay. Think of yourself, it's you I'm sorry for!'

'That's all right! I've got by without your sympathy for the last nineteen years,' Boriska flares up.

'Come on, Boriska, come along now, my friend!' the bald man speaks with sudden gentleness.

'I can't. I know, I know for sure, that it's not the right clay.'

'And what is the "right" clay, then, eh? Well, why don't you tell me?' shouts the caster.

'I know which it is,' repeats Boriska obstinately, head lowered.

'A-a-akh!' the bald man suddenly moans despairingly and, flinging the rag with the clay on to the ground, he turns on his heel and stumbles away over the humps of the field. The boy glares after him, his eyes inflamed and dry, and gulps. His pointed Adam's apple bobs up and down in his thin, birdlike throat.

'All right, then. We'll get by without you!' he yells hoarsely, and marches off in the opposite direction. Andreika is close on his heels. Boriska stops and turns to look again at the caster who is deserting them.

'Look at him! D'you think I want your sort? D'you hear me? I don't want you anyhow if you're like that!' shouts Boriska.

The lads walk straight across the prickly stubble. Boriska is trembling from head to foot. He walks along with his hands tucked into his armpits, in his grotesquely long shirt.

Early one cold morning Boriska is walking through an unmown meadow. He is immediately recognizable in the distance by his funny, bobbing walk. His bast shoes keep falling off his feet, and he has constantly to stop to retie them.

He walks through a young pine grove, crosses a field, and comes out on the bank of a small, quiet stream where he stands for some time on the edge of a cliff, gazing down at the dark water of a creek and the foam going round and round, bewitchingly, over the whirlpool. Then he suddenly gives a sharp kick, and his broken shoe describes an arc, splashes into the swirling water, and begins to spin on one spot, drawn by the whirlpool into a slow, silent giddy-go-round . . .

The boy watches the shoe rotating, and then for some reason decides to fish it out, and starts to make his way down the bank to the water; suddenly he trips, slips, falls down on his behind, and slithers down, his hands clutching at the clay on the bank.

Clay! And what clay! He thrusts his hands deep into it, tears out a lump, squeezes it, breaks it apart and squeezes it again, feels it, caresses it. Fat clay, with no impurities, clear grey, malleable, and thick. This is what he has been longing for. He did not know that this was how it looked, he could not have described it to anyone, because he has never seen it, but he knows now for certain that this is precisely the clay that he needs.

Boriska looks around, smiling blissfully, and shouts: 'Andreika, Semion, Uncle Petia! I've found it!' On the far bank the echo catches his happy yells and carries them over the sad, deserted fields and the yellow-brown woods. Nobody answers.

Rain starts to fall.

Along the muddy road that runs beside the river, on a cart laden with sacks of flour, Andrei Rublëv is driving from the mill. His cowl, cassock and face are powdered with flour. Andrei is sitting on the edge of the cart, his feet dangling, with bast matting over his head as protection from the rain.

He suddenly catches inexplicable, high-pitched shrieks coming from the river. He stops the horse, climbs down from the cart, and walks over to the top of the high bank.

Down below, close to the water, a boy is sitting on the riverside clay, smiling a strange smile, deep in thought, his fingers digging something out from between his bare toes; from time to time he shouts into the empty air, not addressing anybody: 'Stepa-a-an! I've fou-ou-ound it! Andrei-e-ei!'

He knows that nobody is going to answer, and that he is alone; his joyous, thoughtful gaze is fixed on the far bank, towards the distant rust-coloured wood, veiled in a dull film of rain.

Late autumn. In a huge pit, the bed and walls of which are lined with stone, twenty or so artisans are completing the building of the outer clay mould. They are criss-crossing the vast, vaguely bell-shaped pile of clay with iron rods, bent like bows and with hooked ends. Little by little the entire mould is being clad in a mesh, rather like chain-mail.

Up and down the shaky scaffolding scurry workers carrying clay, lime and iron rods.

The bell-casting is a massive undertaking, teeming with people, involving constant din.

Rushing around in the midst of this – at first sight seemingly senseless – hubbub, is the frail, undergrown lad in command of all the workers. He bustles about, doing everything at once, giving out every possible instruction, and occasionally glancing up at the low, overcast sky.

At present he is directing work on the periphery of the pit – in each of the corners huge oak pillars, a metre thick, are being driven into the ground. One has already been dug in and is firmly held in position, and they are about to start work on the second. A shaft as big as a well has already been dug. Several carpenters are chiselling a hole through the top of the pillar for ropes to run through.

Boriska is hovering around the carpenters and, suddenly, unable any longer to watch the measured way in which these self-respecting artisans are working, he pushes one of them aside, grabs the chisel, and starts frenetically chipping away at the wood himself.

At that moment Andreika comes running up to Boriska and calls him aside:

'The merchants won't agree!' he pants.

'What d'you mean, won't agree?' Boriska, soaked in sweat, cannot take it in.

'They're asking for three times as much. They say that for rope like that it's cheap.'

'Buy it then, what else can we do.'

'Boris!' one of the artisans calls his foreman.

'At that price?' says Andreika, alarmed.

'Yes.'

'The Grand Prince'll kill you, we've spent all his money for him already.'

'Boris!' comes the shout from the pit.

'Coming!' Boriska, as he runs off, waves at Andreika in a gesture of desperation. 'I don't care! Buy it!'

Some fifty peasants are all ready to raise the heavy wooden pillar. They are waiting for Boris to give the word.

Andrei Rublëv threads his way through this swarm of people, through the banging and commotion, looking around him, watching all that is going on, stepping aside now for a loaded cart, now for a peasant carrying a beam, now for one of the Prince's horsemen.

'Right, take her up!' yells Boriska. The peasants bend down to the pillar. Boriska walks backwards, concentrating, and steps on Andrei's foot: 'Go away, Father, you'd better go. You could be killed here, crushed!' the boy mutters rapidly, not even looking the monk in the face, and he is on the point of giving another order when someone calls him from the pit.

'Don't put it up without me. I'll be with you directly,' he orders them, and runs down the springy scaffolding into the pit.

'The mould is not going to hold here,' says a bald artisan, pointing to the outer case just above the ground. 'We're going to have to give it another layer of mesh.'

'What d'you mean another layer! I thought you'd already coated it with clay, and you still haven't finished the cope,' he says in surprise.

The bald man gives a condescending laugh. 'You're always in a hurry, aren't you. We've still got to reinforce the cope, and the rods are all finished.'

The lad walks up to the mould, looks it over, and announces:

'That's enough, cover it up, we're not going to do any more rein-forcing. Firing has to start this evening!'

'Is that a joke, or what?' The old, grey-bearded artisan is aston-ished. 'If the mould is not reinforced it won't take the copper, it'll crack, and the whole thing will be lost.'

'And if it snows tomorrow and we don't manage to fire?' says the boy acidly. 'And if we don't manage to fire, won't the work be lost? I'm the one who'll be flogged, not you!'

Rublëv stands on the edge of the pit and gazes down. The artisans, perplexed, are standing on the stone bed of the pit, and among them, constantly on the move, like some restless demon, is this young boy with crazed, limpid eyes.

'I'm not going to do that,' declares the bald man obstinately.

'You're what?' Boriska is rooted to the spot with fury. 'I am telling you to. I am in charge here!'

'There's a gey lot of you in charge here,' grunts the bald man.

The boy stands for a moment looking as if he is about to choke, then shouts at the top of his voice: 'Fiodor!'

An immensely tall fellow, one of the Prince's men, comes run-ning to the pit.

'Flog him!' Boriska points at the bald artisan. 'In the name of the Grand Prince. He's refusing to cast the bell. Not obeying my orders. I'll show you who is in charge here!'

The artisans stand there, dumbfounded. The soldier falls on the artisan and twists his hands behind his back.

'Your father never treated me like this!' shouts the bald man. 'In his name at least – don't shame me in my old age!'

'Oh, so my father comes to mind then, does he?' the boy smiles spitefully, 'Well, you can be flogged in his name!'

Easily, the Prince's man drags the artisan away.

'Now let's finish the mould!' says Boriska, wearily.

The artisans hastily set to work.

Suddenly pale and flagging, with sunken eyes, Boris stands there with his arms hanging down passively; abandoned, alone, he looks miserably up out of the pit at the poplar, bare and dead as it faces winter. A few yellow leaves, still holding on by some miracle, tremble in the blasts of cold wind.

'Boriska! What are you doing? We're still waiting!' The men who have to dig in the pillar are shuffling about on top. The boy sighs heavily: 'Get it in without me.' And walks towards the mould.

With the last of his strength Boriska spreads the cope with clay, alongside the grim-faced casters. Several nights of working with no sleep are taking their toll, and he is falling asleep on his feet, leaning his face up against the wet, oily flank of the mould. An old artisan nudges him in the ribs: 'Go on, go on, have a bit of sleep,' he says, frowning.

Boriska, hardly able to lift his swollen eyelids, staggers like a drunk towards the dilapidated shelter, falls down into the straw and mud, and instantly is engulfed in bottomless darkness, from which he is dragged out immediately by a familiar voice: 'Boriska, Boriska, wake up! Boriska!'

He just manages to open his gummy eyes and sees that all around him is as white as white. No mud, no grey, dead grass. From the sky fall enormous, downy snowflakes. The old artisan is shaking him by the shoulder: 'Get up! It's snowing. I've started firing.'

Boriska jumps up, holding on to his trousers, and dashes towards the pit, scolding the artisan as he goes: 'Why did you do it without me? What right had you? I am the one who knows when it has to be done.'

He runs up to the pit, and stops, amazed, still not fully awake, clinging with both hands to his trousers to stop them falling down. A tall, powerful flame, roaring and furious, is licking upwards, touching with its sharp tongues the twilit, darkening sky. Snow goes on falling.

Winter. Work on the bell is in full swing. The tall, thick pillars are long since in place at the corners of the black, charred pit where the mould is already prepared. The pillars stand not vertically, but leaning very slightly over the pit so that they will not budge when the mould or the bell are hauled up. A lime-bark roof has been set over the mould as a shelter from the snow. The great multitude of people working round the pit is now bigger than ever. The construction of four casting furnaces, placed between the pillars, is nearing completion.

From every direction sledge tracks converge on the site, and along them metals are being brought and put in a huge pile for smelting. Carts crawl along with copper pigs, heavy lumps of copper from old bells are dragged over with ropes. The lumps are clumsy and heavy, clustered around each are some thirty or even forty peasants, and soldiers of the Prince's army.

Boriska is busy at the scales, weighing the silver as it is delivered, and around him stand the artisans and soldiers who brought it here.

'Too little silver!' Boriska tells a soldier firmly. 'Tell the Prince not to stint, he hasn't sent enough.'

'We've never known the Grand Prince stint over anything,' the Prince's lieutenant, Stepan, retorts with an angry scowl.

'I don't know anything about that! We need another half-pood!' declares Boriska categorically.

'What difference is it going to make,' – the bald craftsman grins – 'half a pood here or there when the bell is going to weigh five thousand.'

'And who knows the secret of bell copper? You or I?' Boriska flares up. They are all silent.

'So tell the Grand Prince that he is not to stint, look how much silver people have collected, without even being asked.' Boriska nods towards a pile of silver objects, vessels and ornaments. 'We need another half-pood.' Boriska turns away, climbs down into the black pit and, going up to the men working at the bottom, he grins broadly.

'What's up with you?' asks Andreika.

'I can get all the silver I want out of the Prince.' He claps his hand over his mouth, rolls his eyes, and looks round, pretending to be scared that someone might have heard him. 'And the bell still won't ring!' And he bursts out laughing, a gurgling, hysterical laugh. The workmen are embarrassed, and look away. Boriska looks up and sees, on the edge of the pit, the Grand Prince. He is seated on a white stallion and his steady, serious gaze is fixed on the boy.

'You had better be careful!' he says in a quiet, menacing tone, and, turning his horse, he rides away.

Boriska sits down on the ground, dismayed. Two crows take off noiselessly from the snow-covered poplar, and large flakes of snow come floating quietly down from its black branches . . .

Another spring. A flock of rooks, unable to recognize their native haunts, circle in the sky.

The workmen are busy by the furnaces which hum on a low, threatening note. The metal is being smelted. The whole site is filled with people. The carpenters are constructing huge gates with the help of which the finished bell will be hoisted up. From each furnace a gutter runs to the mould, for the molten metal to flow down.

Boriska is thinner; he is utterly preoccupied, and he frowns, as he walks up to one of the four furnaces.

'Well?' he asks, brusque and impatient.

The sweating caster, his hair held back by a strap, looks as if he might be melting in the heat; he answers with a smile: 'I told you it couldn't be less than three days. Look at all the copper that's got to be boiled up!'

'It's already three days,' Boriska says quietly, dropping his eyes. 'You make sure . . .'

'No, lad,' the sweating peasant wipes his face. 'It won't be ready before tonight.'

Boriska looks up sharply and snaps: 'What have I told you!'

The peasant's expression changes, he deftly knocks open the red-hot door of the furnace and, screwing up his eyes in the blinding, scorching light, pokes the molten copper with a rod, then jumps backwards off the little step, slams the door shut, and says glumly: 'I said it would be ready by tonight . . .'

The boy walks away, deep in thought biting his lip. His eyes wander over to the trunk of the poplar, now green with buds, and with last year's black nests in its branches; above them the flock of rooks wheel anxiously, unable to recognize their own tree.

Night. The brilliantly flashing flames illumine the bell pit. Round the smoking, red-hot furnaces the workers with their soot-blackened faces look like demons. The whole site is filled with a menacing roar that drowns all other sound. In the open doors of the furnace the molten copper shines like the sun. The casters' red-hot iron rods trace elaborate patterns in the darkness.

Boriska is stirring copper in one of the furnaces. Andreika runs up to him.

'The second and third furnaces are ready.'

The sweating face of the long-haired caster appears out of the darkness.

'Mine's ready!'

'Go on, go on, it's all ready!' Boriska hurries the old artisan away from the fourth furnace. The lad looks round at the craftsmen and now for the first time he notices that the whole site is ringed around with a crowd a thousand strong, as if the whole of Moscow had come to see his work. The poplar is hanging with small boys who are staring with enchanted faces and open mouths at the mysteriously synchronized activity seething below them. Boriska's throat contracts with excitement. His breath is coming in deep gasps.

'Well! All set! Well? Are we going?' The old artisan shouts, almost with despair. Boriska moistens his dry, trembling lips with his tongue, he only has strength enough to nod his head, barely perceptibly.

The casters dash to the furnaces and knock open the lower flues, and the shining, seething metal rushes down the chutes and into the mould, with a song that is unlike any other sound, a whistling howl, a low, hooting polyphony. And now the mould starts to echo as it fills, a gigantic vessel into which clear liquid silver is being poured.

As Boris, his head on one side, listens intently to the thunderous music of this molten mass of silver and copper, he shudders with the tension that is tearing his heart, and within himself he cries out, ecstatic, choking with joy: 'Pour! Hu-u-urra-a-ay! A-a-a-a! Lord, help us! Let it be all right! Po-o-o-ur!'

A crowd of people in long, black garments come running along the dark road, panting and stumbling. They run up the slope at the top of which stands the poplar, bathed in a flickering, uneven light by the flames on the molten metal, and push their way through the dense wall of people towards the pit.

These are the monks of the Monastery of the Saviour and St Andronnikus. At their head is Rublëv. Breathing heavily he pushes his way to the front, and glances anxiously around the site until he notices Boriska, hunched up beside a furnace; and his face lights up.

Evening. The pit is cooling, and the artisans are standing at the bottom, around the enormous black mound. The cracked, charred mould imparts its heat to the frosty air that streams above it like water.

Boriska, stupefied, black, is the first to go up to the mould and, with a crow-bar, knocks a lump of it away. Following his lead the others start to break up the mould.

Boriska throws himself into his work. He chips away the baked earth, tears apart the wire mesh, crumbles the clay that has been baked as hard as stone. The pieces fall to the ground with a clatter. His hand, holding the crow-bar, freezes in mid-air. Staring at Boriska is the awesome, carbonized, copper face of St George.

Darkness is falling. The bell, enormous, dirty, black, stands in the pit, and around it the artisans are sitting on the warm fragments of the mould.

'Well, tomorrow we're going to have a day of it!' The old craftsman sighs. 'Why don't we get some sleep, eh?'

The men stand up. Only Boriska remains sitting, leaning against the warm, rough surface of the bell.

'Boriska! Come on!'

The lad, without opening his eyes, moves his lips like a child, and mutters thickly, as if trying to justify himself: 'Just coming, in a minute, I'll . . . here . . .' And he falls asleep, his cheek pressed against his own, mute child.

The men climb up the scaffolding. The bald fellow yawns and turns to the old man: 'I just can't understand how the Grand Prince could have trusted him to do it . . . I can't understand it . . .'

At last the long-awaited day dawns.

From early morning the land around the pit has been packed with people, and more are arriving all the time. In every direction, as far as the eye can see, the site is surrounded by crowds. Everyone from Moscow and the surrounding villages want to witness this event, the like of which happens only once or twice in a lifetime.

Thick ropes run from the bell through pulleys set in the pillars, to the gates. By each of the gates thirty peasants stand waiting for the signal. Boriska is in the pit by the bell, amongst the craftsmen. He is abstracted, as if he were under sentence of death.

'Well? What are we doing?' the old artisan asks Boriska in a serious, businesslike voice. He is terribly anxious. 'Yes . . . yes . . .' Boriska replies, equally seriously, and inappropriately.

'Ready? Do we start?' goes on the old man. 'Then wave. Go on, wave your hand!'

The men, having checked for the last time that everything has been made fast, climb up from the pit which has become more a part of them than their own homes. Boriska, his pale lips pressed together, waves his arm.

Hundreds of arms are tensed simultaneously, hands clamped on the handles of the gates, faces are suffused, veins stand out. The mighty ropes stretch and sing like the strings of an instrument. And not a single person amongst all those gathered around the pit is indifferent or detached as they wait for the new bell, invested with so many hopes, to come up out of the earth.

Now the top can be seen above the pit. Slowly, as if unwillingly, swaying majestically, it starts to grow, and all the people watching are filled with wonder and joy.

Laboriously, with unimagined difficulty, the bell rises over the earth and several dozen peasants dash to thrust thick beams under it, so that if anything goes wrong it cannot fall back down.

Boriska is moving as if in his sleep; the craftsmen are all busy, each with his own job, and he wanders among them in a daze, constantly under their feet and in everyone's way.

At last all is ready. The ropes are tied, the bell is hanging safely, the tongue, weighing many poods, is tied back. The Archbishop in his vestments and all the clergy have taken up their places. They are waiting for the Grand Prince.

One of the Prince's lieutenants, in ceremonial costume, rides up to the craftsmen and tells them: 'The Grand Prince will be here shortly. He was delayed by a foreign ambassador.'

And now a colourful cavalcade emerges from the Kremlin gates. The Grand Prince and his foreign guest ride at the head on different-coloured stallions. They are followed by a vast, richly clad suite.

The crowd part to let the Prince through, bowing down to the ground. The Grand Prince and the foreign guest ride up to the pit and stop. The craftsmen stand in a group, in silence. At last the senior man anxiously gives Boriska a sharp, surreptitious nudge forward. Bewildered, hardly able to put one shaky foot in front of the other, head lowered, he walks towards the Grand Prince and stops some paces from him, bows awkwardly, rather to one side, and does not look up.

The Prince peers at him and turns to the ambassador. 'Look at the craftsmen I have in charge!'

The foreigner is tall with clean-shaven, beautifully tended cheeks and marvellous upturned, curling moustaches, and wears a starched white cambric collar on a black shirt, a gold dagger and a huge hat with a plume – no one has ever seen such splendour. But nobody is taking the slightest notice of him.

The ambassador smiles politely, leaning to one side as he listens to his interpreter, and then turns to the Prince nodding emphatically. He has not in fact understood a word.

Still smiling, the Prince says: 'Well, I am ready.'

Boriska cannot hear or see. Only when the lieutenant rides up to him and hisses urgently through his teeth: 'Go on, go on, blockhead . . .' does he obediently turn round and walk towards the bell.

Boriska meekly takes up his place. The strapping peasant caster with the leather band round his hair whispers without turning his head, excited, mocking: 'Well, are you going to swing her or shall I give a hand?' He furtively crosses himself, walks towards the bell, and takes hold of the rope attached to the tongue.

A sigh ripples over the crowd, and then a fraught, unnatural silence descends.

Slowly, inexorably, the great, heavy tongue starts to swing.

It swings wider and wider, further and further out of control.

The Grand Prince stands like a statue, turned to stone in his saddle.

The artisans are staring at the ground, averting their eyes from the tongue as it swings wider and wider, the only sense alive in them at this moment is hearing, and they wait for the sound for the sake of which they have been working for an entire year, like men cursed, enduring shame and humiliation, not knowing themselves why they trusted this fanatical boy.

Boriska watches the swinging heavy tongue, he is wide-eyed and unflinching, but his legs suddenly give way and he sinks to the ground.

Ten poods of tongue are swinging almost to the wall of the bell. Once more . . . once more . . . Nearer and nearer to the heavy, mysterious, mute copper . . .

A tremendous, dense, low sound breaks slowly away from the

startled bell and floats, tranced, out to the furthest edges of the transfixed, silent crowd.

The next stroke awakens a peal in many voices, and then answers it in a disorderly, joyous carillon.

People wave in high delight, shout, take off their caps, turn to the cupolas of the Kremlin and cross themselves.

And the bell hums and hums, smoothly gathering power, the ringer is swinging the heavy tongue further and further, and shouting ecstatically at the top of his voice.

The Grand Prince twitches his nose, and turns away from the glaring spring sun. The foreigner has taken off his hat and is looking around smiling, and making a play of flinching at the deafening, relentless roar.

Boriska rises from the ground and takes a desperate gulp of cold spring air; he walks, without looking where he is going, with both hands on the back of his head, ruffling his coarse hair, and people stand aside to let him pass, gazing at him with curious, incredulous admiration. Uncontrolled, happy tears are pouring down his boyish face, which is contorted with sobs.

He stumbles, and a pair of hands seize him. Choking with tears he presses up against a chest that smells of smoke and peasant sweat, and he hears a strange, hoarse voice, comforting and hard to understand: 'It's all right . . . it doesn't matter . . . it's all over . . . it's finished . . . it's all right now . . . all is well . . .'

'The bastard . . . my father, the bloody monster.' Boriska is suffocating with his tears. 'The filthy skinflint . . . He never told me the secret, he died, without ever telling me . . .'

'And look how it has turned out . . . it's all fine.' Andrei with trembling hands strokes the lad's hair and his thin neck, and his back, as skinny as an adolescent. He looks up and his eyes meet the gaze of a figure in an old Tartar kaftan with a skull-cap on his shaven head. It is Daniil.

A still spring evening. The fields are deserted and melancholy, here and there lie patches of half-thawed snow. Four figures are walking along the road towards the Trinity Monastery: Andrei and Daniil at the front, and a little way behind them their apprentices – Mikhail, once the blind men's guide, aged sixteen, and another, younger, boy in a cast-off homespun coat which is far too big for him.

Along the roadside are bedraggled-looking birches with rooks' nests tangled in their branches. The rooks are calling and arguing, as they settle down for the night in trees that stand motionless in the cold air.

It is freezing slightly, but the road is dotted with long puddles which mirror the light evening sky.

'Tired?' Andrei asks Daniil.

'Not at all.'

'From that tree over there you can see it all.'

'What?'

'From the top you can see the whole of the Holy Trinity, as if it were lying in the palm of your hand.'

'A-a-h . . . So we're nearly there.'

'I remember once, I fell off it . . . It doesn't seem to have grown, somehow!'

'Maybe it wasn't that tree at all? Maybe you're muddling it with another?'

Andrei is very excited, and his excitement is making him almost garrulous, unnaturally animated.

'Those rooks, just look at them all!' Andrei looks up and smiles a joyful smile.

'D'you remember how many there used to be at the Trinity?' Daniil recalls.

'Oh yes,' interrupts Andrei, 'but as soon as you get beyond Kliazma there are just thousands of them! They're lovely . . . And I wonder – are they the same ones or not?'

Daniil does not understand, he looks at Andrei.

'I wonder whether they are the same rooks as the year before?'

'Probably, I don't know.' Daniil smiles dismissively.

'And what drags them back here year after year? Why don't they live over there in their warm countries! But no, back they come . . .'

They walk for a time in silence.

'Never mind, we'll soon be there, and the first thing we'll do is have a bath after our journey,' says Daniil. 'Ye-es . . . The Brothers . . . I don't suppose any of the old ones are left . . .'

'If only we could get that kind of group together again, Daniil! Piotr, Sergei, Grishka, Aleksei, Foma!' Andrei remembers them. Daniil shakes his head: 'No, Foma . . .'

'No, no, he was quite right . . . He did what he felt was right. He had integrity, that lad, don't you talk about him in that tone . . . How many are no longer with us, Lord, God Almighty!'

'Look, there's that oak over there, d'you remember?' Daniil points to a bare, black oak close to the road.

'That one there?'

'We sheltered from the rain under it, and I was telling you about the Maiden's Field.'

'Oh, yes . . . when we were leaving . . .'

Suddenly Andrei stops and says quietly, looking wearily to one side: 'Perhaps we should go back, Daniil?'

'What do you mean, back?' Daniil stops in dismay, in the middle of the road.

The apprentices follow, walking on opposite sides of the road, and crunching through the thin film of ice that is beginning to cover the puddles.

'I know what they're talking about,' says Mishka.

'Who? Them?' asks the younger boy.

'Of course, who else. They're scared.'

'Scared of what?'

'What d'you think? They're old, they're scared they've forgotten.'

'Oh, come on,' says the younger boy with conviction, 'they couldn't be. Rublëv is a master, he's second to none!'

'Not painting for ten years is enough to make anyone forget.'

'Then why did you get yourself apprenticed to him?' asks the other, mocking.

'Of course he's a great master.' Mishka squats down on his haunches beside a puddle. It reflects the twilit sky and the bare branches of the trees. 'A superb master . . . Only . . . Only now painting has to be quite different.'

'How different?' the boy asks, puzzled, squatting down beside Mishka.

'Different.'

'And does Andrei know how to do it?'

Mishka sighs and shakes his head vaguely.

'Then you should tell him,' suggests the younger one wickedly.

'I shall tell him . . . when the time comes.'

'Hey, come here!' Andrei's voice reaches them.

The boys exchange glances, worried that they may have been overheard, then they get up and hurry to catch up with Andrei and Daniil.

'Stop dawdling about, walk with us,' says Andrei when the two, their hearts sinking, catch up with them by the oak tree.

The four of them walk slowly along the road in silence. Then Daniil, pursuing their earlier conversation, turns to Andrei: 'What about Theophanes? It was he who kept saying, "I've had enough, I've had enough of being alive!" Then you remember when he was dying, how he wept! "If only I could live just a little longer, just a tiny bit, and go on painting . . ."'

'Maybe . . .' Andrei looks around, nonplussed. In place of the monastery pine woods in the distance stand black, bare hills.

'I don't understand,' mutters Andrei. 'Those hills . . . and where is the wood?'

'Yes.' Daniil stops and looks around. 'We seem to have gone wrong.'

'Which way should we go then? We started out the right way.'

'Look, what's that?' asks Daniil.

Ahead of them, actually on the road, flickers a small fire. Two figures are seated by the fire, their faces dimly lit up by its glow.

'Let's go and ask,' suggests Andrei.

'God-fearing people are at home now, what are they doing here, in the middle of the countryside . . .' wonders Daniil, not budging.

Andrei smiles.

'We can't have lost our way.' Daniil plays for time.

'We're not going to walk through the mud in order to avoid

them.' Andrei laughs softly, and walks towards the light. The others follow him.

Beside the fire sit two men: one little fellow, and a great strapping peasant with a coal-black beard and a grim expression. They are gazing into the dying flames in silence.

'You won't drive us away, good folk?' Andrei says by way of greeting, as he approaches the fire.

The little man looks round.

'Why would we stop you . . . warming yourselves,' and he moves aside to make room for the travellers.

The ikon painters come up to the fire.

'No, we have to be moving on . . . Is it far still to the Holy Trinity?' asks Andrei.

'To the Holy Trinity?' repeats the little one, and looks at the travellers, his eyes attentive and merry. He has a curious enunciation: instead of 't' and 'd' he produces something half-way between 's' and 'l'. 'Over there, the other side of those hills, you'll see the monastery. You're practically there.'

'Where's the wood gone?' says Daniil in surprise.

'They cut it down, about five years back . . . If you were to come back again in ten years you'd not find anything left at all.' The little man smiles.

Andrei, disturbed, stares into his face, and listens to his voice, catching something forgotten and familiar. And as the little man stretches out his hands to the fire and leans forward, Andrei recognizes him as the buffoon. That very buffoon whom Kirill once denounced. Daniil recognizes him as well, and the two of them exchange glances.

'Have you not been to these parts for some time then?' asks the buffoon with interest.

'Not for a long time,' answers Daniil.

'Neither have I.' The buffoon nods in the direction of the silent bearded man. 'We only arrived today.'

'So you're alive?' remarks Andrei.

'And why would I not be?' The buffoon is puzzled.

'D'you not remember us then?' Andrei nods at Daniil. 'We were there when you were . . . You remember, when the Prince's men came. You'd been singing.'

'A-a-h,' the buffoon utters vaguely, looking into their faces. 'I don't remember, somehow. I remember the Prince's men all right, but not you!' He laughs.

'And there were two peasants fighting, and you and I separated them,' Andrei reminds him.

'A-ah, yes, yes.' The buffoon nods, but it is obvious that he does not remember either Andrei or Daniil. 'Somebody denounced me that day,' he says, and yawns, making the sign of the cross over his mouth.

'And I know who did it. I knew him,' says Andrei.

'He's dead now,' adds Daniil.

'What difference does it make,' says the buffoon cheerfully to Andrei. 'If it wasn't him then it was you, or him.' He nods towards Daniil. 'There'll always be someone ready to betray you, it's of no matter.'

Andrei and Daniil say nothing. The two apprentices are gazing wide-eyed at the buffoon and drinking in his every word.

'Why don't you sit yourselves down,' he says expansively.

'No, thanks. We have to be at the monastery as soon as possible.' Daniil frowns.

'Where were you all this time?' asks Andrei.

'I spent twenty years in the Belozersk wasteland. It was a good spot, beautiful country, only chilly in the pit. It wasn't too bad when there were two or three of you, but on your own . . .' the buffoon makes a dismissive gesture.

'So you're not performing any more?'

'No, how could I?' The little man laughs. 'The first thing they did was cut off half my tongue! No, I've given it up, forgotten how to do it.'

Andrei is too upset to utter a word. He looks away from the serenely smiling buffoon to his companion, who is sitting saying nothing, staring intently into the fire, not blinking, like a fire-worshipper.

Andrei clears his throat, embarrassed, and says: 'But you sang well . . .'

'It would depend.' The buffoon smiles. 'Sometimes I would dance and sing with all that was in me – I could do anything. When I struck up a complaint, I'd have them all rolling about with laughter! And then at other times something would come over me, and I wouldn't be able to utter a word, let alone dance or sing . . . my spirits would be that low . . .' The buffoon rakes together the dying embers with his foot and adds: 'Yes . . . I've forgotten it all.'

'Oh, no, you can't have,' says Daniil with conviction.

'I was asked to go to the Grand Prince, you know, as his jester. His jester had died. And I refused . . . What do I want with the Grand Prince, I'd do better as a carpenter . . .'

They are all silent. The buffoon looks into the fire for a time, smiling. Then he stands up and says to his companion: 'Come on, brother, time we were off . . .'

The bearded fellow starts, stands up in silence, and goes off into the darkness.

'Aren't you afraid when it's so dark?' Andrei asks the buffoon. He raises his eyebrows, astonished.

'What about you?'

'Why should I be afraid?'

'You're a queer one . . . In that case, why should I?' The buffoon glances round into the darkness and then turns to the ikon painters.

'Thank you, good folk, for your loving kindness.'

He bows from the waist, and follows his bearded companion.

Daniil stares into the darkness and shouts cheerfully after him: 'You're pretty cheerful after those twenty years!'

Out of the darkness comes an answering laugh from the buffoon, and his shout: 'You've not seen the half of it!'

The monks turn, and start off along the frozen muddy road towards the monastery.

Through the stillness of the night comes a lingering, sad Russian song.

The buffoon is singing.

Tender pale blue and ash-grey patches emerge and melt, coming out of the darkness of extinguished fire, pulsating and succeeding one another in steady sequence. Emerald splashes and hot ochre, cracked in the course of five hundred years . . .

Soft modulations of unimaginable ochre and golds, like autumn woods bathed in sunlight, spaces, the blue of the sky which has given its colour to the folds of garments falling and frozen in abrupt contours, mother-of-pearl tenderness of opaque brush-strokes, light, misty blue, like distant forest, pomegranate pink, like a September aspen leaf, dull mauve, somehow reminiscent of dark, deep water covered in ripples, auguring bad weather . . .

Woven into the smokey, pure splashes, the very translucency of which is appealing, are the precise, measured decorations of the frescoes. Lines and contours repeat and multiply, converge and interweave, meet and eliminate one another, with deliberate lack of sequence.

Gently bending arms like magical French curves, veils that seem to be filled with wind and finish in sudden folds, like crushed tin . . .

The Last Judgement. The sorceress, in her ordinary peasant woman's sarafan, has wet, heavy, flowing hair. She is holding a ship in her triumphantly raised hand, holding it easily, and her expression is full of meaning, for that ship is neither more nor less than the souls of those who have perished on the waters.

And the splash of water can be heard, and, muffled by the mist, the yearning call, without hope and full of grief: 'Marfa-a-a! Swii-i-m! Ma-a-arfa!'

Solemn and sorrowful, the faces of the righteous women float past, and the regular, muffled blows of the Tartar sabre ring out through the tense silence.

Beautiful, pretty, ugly, the faces of these women have been taken by Andrei, and, on the authority of a sublime whim of liberated imagination, elevated into the throng of the Righteous.

On and on the women walk in a sorrowful procession, hoping for salvation through this civic death, and the dull blows of the sharpened Tartar sabre sound like a heart-beat . . .

Ikons and frescoes float past us one after the other, limpid and severe, tender and harsh at the same time . . .

And, synchronous with what we see, the ear catches the music of nature, intimately bound with the design for the paintings: and it allows us to understand the path Andrei travelled to bring that design to fulfilment, showing it to have been utterly simple. For it is the music that Andrei heard during those moments when supreme, radiant images were coming into being within him.

Solemnity of line and nobility of colour, born in pain, in the state of being in love with people, give way to battle-sounds, to the crackle and roar of conflagration, the tender buzz of bees over snow-white fields of buckwheat – the song of the earth, which compelled Andrei to love azure blue, turquoise tinges, the joyous juxtaposition of ochre cliffs and the heavy blue weight of angels' robes.

And finally: *The Trinity*, the meaning and culmination of Andrei's life. Serene, noble, filled with breathless joy in the face of human brotherhood. A single being physically divided into three, and a triple union, revealing amazing singleness of mind in the face of a future that stretches on through the centuries.

The hand movements are measured and harmonious; in the depths of the attentive eyes lies a tragic understanding of the essence of the human vocation, contained in the beautiful, unconscious search for the ideal.

The rhythm of the garments falling freely from the shoulders, the contours flying smoothly and slowly, sliding over the blue surface, the colour of cornflowers, now beginning to accumulate pale mauve and smokey purple, criss-crossed with the web of cracks left by the centuries, which only enhances the utter beauty of the ikon; or abruptly repeating the angles of the yellow hill, where a pine stands by the tawny-russet planes of stone cliffs.

Again and again our ears are filled with the echo of a time that has died, reminding us of the minutes of Rublëv's inspiration, those moments when his astonishing designs were born.

And now between the camera and the light sky of *The Trinity* with its vestiges of gold burst drops of rain, isolated at first and then becoming more frequent, until they merge into a gleaming, pouring flood, shot through by the lightning of a distant storm. We hear the even, monotonous sound of rain.

The camera pans from the blurred, streaming ikon, and we see meadows grey with rain, a bend in a river, rippling, lead-grey, in the wind, and horses standing mournfully in the rain on the wet grass at the water's edge.